OBSTRUCTED VIEW

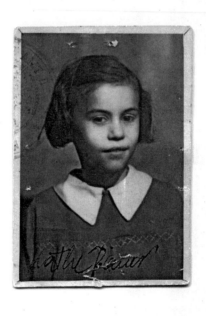

Obstructed View

A Memoir of a Young Girl Growing Up
in Wartime Vienna

Katharina Rich Perlow

ISBN: 0615926290

ISBN 13: 9780615926292

Dedicated to the memory of
Mama and Maxi

CONTENTS

TABLE OF CONTENTS

TO THE READER

Now and then, through the years, when someone would ask me, "Where were you during the war?" I often avoided the question. Whenever I tried to tell the story, I always got very emotional—and quickly found I had to abandon it before the end. But as these requests have been repeated over and over, I have come to realize that I must do my best to write it down, especially for my children and grandchildren to know my story.

The quiet terror of my childhood was something I was never able to visit without great emotion. When I tried to tell my story to friends and family, I was unable to find the strength or the right words to recount the past. Many people assumed I had escaped Vienna somehow, perhaps by the child transports bound for England at the time or by obtaining visas to America or another country open to emigrants. No one could conceive that I actually survived the war in Vienna in plain sight.

I feel I need to remind my readers that this is a very personal story. Many of the events in this memoir occurred when I was between the ages of six and thirteen. To that I can add many of the things I heard repeated over and over again in conversations with my family and with other survivors of the war. And I recently discovered that my brother, Max, also took it upon himself to commit to paper some notes telling our story. I have incorporated some of these invaluable writings throughout my tale, filling in gaps that might otherwise have been lost.

There is much that I have left out, and for that I apologize. I have done my best to recall everything I can, but I know there were many events happening at the time that I was too young to understand, or were not discussed in my presence, so there are necessarily gaps where I am unable to give an exact report of what occurred. When you read, "I don't know" or "I can't remember," you will know why.

I should also note that I started to write this story many years ago. In the intervening years, I have been quite busy with my career, raising children and running my own fine arts gallery, The Katharina Rich Perlow Gallery, from 1984 to 2011. So some details may have faded with the passage of time. But there are things that a child cannot possibly forget—events that are almost as vivid to me now as when they happened. You will note that the most dramatic situations I remember quite well. They were traumatic. And they cannot be forgotten.

• • • • •

The love and encouragement of my daughters Monica and Irina, and my husband, Bill, have enabled me to finally tell my story. I am grateful to them, and also to Ed Claflin and Dennis Ambrose for helping me find the right words and to reach back into my memories. I am most thankful to my editor and angel-at-large, Dennis Ambrose, for his patience, his calm, always giving the right advice, and encouraging me to publish my story.

—Katharina Rich Perlow

OBSTRUCTED VIEW

CHAPTER 1

Wiener Neustadt 1938—the Family

THOUGH I CAN REMEMBER VERY LITTLE BEFORE the age of six, I do know that one point of contention between Mama and me was the issue of my nap time. She insisted that I take a nap every morning, but I was an active child and sleep didn't interest me. Yet I knew better than to defy my mother's wishes. Her will prevailed.

We did reach a compromise, however, acceptable to both of us. I would take a nap as she wished if she would let me lie down on the bench in the kitchen. Certainly a hard wooden bench was not the most comfortable resting place. But it offered something that even the coziest down mattress could not have matched—the warmth of the kitchen, the bustling-about of my beautiful mother as she sliced vegetables or prepared her delicious poppy-seed dumplings. The heady fragrance of my mother's cooking filled the room.

My sister, Lilly, who was more than two years older than me, often went to play with a girlfriend across the street from our apartment. Since she refused to take her little sister along, the kitchen was temporarily my domain.

That kitchen bench, then, is what I remember best about my six-year-old self in the Austrian city of Wiener Neustadt in 1938. Outside the walls of our apartment, terrible things were beginning to happen—events that I would not fully understand for many years to come. In the warmth of my mother's kitchen, I felt completely safe, protected, and secure.

But in 1938, safety was an illusion.

· · · · ·

My mother, Agnes, born in 1892, came from a Catholic family that had a farm in the town of Zagersdorf, Burgenland, a place not farther than about fifty kilometers from Vienna. It is a wide flat area, ringed with large meadows with wheat, corn, poppy flowers, and many vineyards. Mama grew up speaking both Croatian and German. There were eight in her family. By the age of seventeen, Agnes was considered the village beauty. And she was gainfully employed, walking eight kilometers almost daily to the town of Stoettera, another village near Eisenstadt (a town well known as the birthplace of the Austrian composer Haydn). There she babysat for another family of eight, the Bauers, who were Orthodox Jews.

It was unthinkable to both families that the babysitter would fall in love with Josef (nicknamed Peppie). He was seven years older than Agnes and the youngest sibling of the Bauer family. But fall in love she did.

Since I have few documents from that time, I cannot say whether there was a formal wedding of any kind, though it seems unlikely. What I do know is that there were at least two marriage certificates, one from my father's town, one from my mother's. They are both dated 1931—just a year before I was born—but that postdates the birth of my brother, Maximilian (Max), who was born in 1924, and Karoline (Lilly), born in 1930. As I imagine it, then, my father and mother avoided the whole issue of interfaith marriage by simply living together (in very modern style) in the relative urban anonymity of Wiener Neustadt, which was only about forty kilometers from their respective birthplaces. There, they raised their first two children as if they were already married, legitimizing the arrangement a year before I came along.

In accord with Jewish tradition, all their children were named after deceased relatives. I was given the name of my grandmother Katharina (who died when my father was only two years old), and my sister was named Karoline after my father's sister (who had died at an early age). From the start, there was no question about how the children would be raised. We were Jewish. My mother thought "Karoline" and "Katharina" were old-fashioned names, though, and so she therefore ended up calling my sister "Lilly" and me "Kaethe"—which seemed to her more up-to-date.

As for any possible reconciliation between their families, it simply did not occur. My mother converted to Judaism and would not be reconciled with any of her family again until after my father's death. On the Bauer side, my grandfather was so adamantly opposed to marriage outside the faith that he continued to insist, almost to his deathbed, that my mother could not possibly be a shiksa even though Uncle Wilhelm, my father's brother, bluntly told him so. (The truth was blurted out by Uncle Wilhelm in the midst of a confrontation between the two of them.) It was simply unthinkable that a Bauer would insult the family by marrying a non-Jew.

The Bauers, the only Jews in Stoettera, were the prosperous owners of the village's only country store. It was like most other country stores of the time, offering everything for sale that was not produced by the farmers themselves, from carton food like sugar, rice, coffee, and candies to fabric, matches, shoelaces, and much more. (This store would remain in the family after my grandfather's death at age ninety-one. His unmarried daughter, my Aunt Rosa, took over the store and ran it until it was eventually confiscated by the Nazis in 1938.)

Before the war, the Bauer family was well assimilated with other residents of Stoettera, and they spoke the same village dialect as the other village people. All the boys in the family got good educations. My father was sent to school in Shopron, Hungary, where he became fluent in Hungarian as well as German. Like his brothers, he subsequently became a successful businessman, importing food products and coal from Hungary to Austria. In those early days, I am told, my father was warm, handsome, exciting, always very well dressed, quite well-to-do—and he loved to race motorcycles.

Weekends, he and my mother drove to the elegant resort of Am Semmering, less than an hour from Wiener Neustadt. The serpentine road leading up the mountains was ideal for motorcycle racing. The young couple must have spent many wonderful weekends traveling to and from the resort. Once children came along, of course, their outings became more sedate.

My father, Josef Bauer. The date of this photo is unknown, but it probably shows him in his thirties.

Unfortunately, as I was to learn later, my father also loved to gamble. At first we had all lived in a very nice house in Wiener Neustadt, but as my father's gambling debts caught up with him, we were forced to downsize to a second-floor apartment where my earliest memories occur. Of course, as a child under six, I knew nothing about my father's gambling habit or the looming threat of family indigence. What I valued most about my father at that time was his comforting presence and the way he would protect my siblings and me from my mother's occasional outbursts of wrath. For there were times when her disciplinary side took over, and we would be reprimanded in scorching tones for our unruly ways. Father stepped in to calm the waters by spreading out his arms, and we would hide behind them. It was like a spontaneous game of "come-get-me-if-you-can" that served as a cooling-off period until Mama's mood had passed.

Whatever my father's financial circumstances, he remained on very good terms with his siblings. Fortunately for all of us, those well-to-do uncles and aunts readily opened their doors to everyone in my family. My Uncle Wilhelm, also living in Wiener Neustadt, owned a successful wholesale dry goods business and was especially kind to us. Almost every day after school, Max would stop and visit Uncle Wilhelm's to do his homework there, play chess with his son, our cousin Ernoe, and stay for dinner. There was a particularly close relationship between Ernoe and Max. Ernoe was a few years older than Max, and it was he who introduced my brother to opera, which would become a life-long passion for Max and an influence on all of us for the rest of our lives.

Many summers, after the end of each school year, Max was invited to stay with Aunt Rosa in Stoettera. He made friends with some of the village children of his own age.

• • • • •

Among other friends in the city of Wiener Neustadt were the children of the Buchsbaum family—Max, Julie, and Fritz. Fritz was my age, and I think he may have had a crush on me. I, in turn, liked him, especially because he had a scooter, and I was dying to ride it.

My sister, Lilly, was best friends with Fritz's sister, Julie. They were the same age, and they loved to sew clothing for their little miniature celluloid dolls. As they became more skilled as seamstresses, they also became more ambitious. One day when they were only nine years old, I saw them secretly trying to sew brassieres for themselves.

The Buchsbaums' son Max was just a little bit younger than my brother, and it seemed possible the two might become friends. But the friendship never developed, and I now think this was because the two had very little in common. Already, my brother had become quite sophisticated in his thinking, and Max Buchsbaum was just a regular, normal kid for his age, without the interests in reading and music that were beginning to preoccupy my brother.

In those days, there were no ready-made clothes, so we relied on Frau Buchsbaum, an amateur seamstress, for some of our wardrobe. Unfortunately, since I had a sister who was just a little more than two years older, I was mostly consigned to accept her hand-me-downs. But once Frau Buchsbaum made a winter coat that was just for me, and one that I urgently needed. I should have been pleased, but unfortunately it was a brown chunk of clothing that did not suit me at all. I'm sure it had great utility value: winters were cold, and we always got a lot of snow. But I hated the way it made me look—like an overstuffed, clumsy brown bear. And I was only a skinny little kid!

Looking at one photograph that I have of my mother, taken when she was thirty years old, it is quite obvious that her wardrobe did not come from the same source as mine. She must have had her clothes made by a real seamstress, probably at a salon. In the photo Mama's dark silk outer jacket is neatly tailored. Underneath, worn like a camisole, is a delicate white lace blouse with a beautiful fringe. In this photo, in fact, she looks very much the modern woman with her dark hair pulled back in a tight bun. What comes back to me, even now, is the wonderful fresh scent of the cream (always touched with a light shading of powder) that she put on her cheeks whenever she was going out. (Years later, when we lived in Vienna, she would make special trips to Wiener Neustadt to buy that same scented cream from the local Apotheke near our former apartment. In the years after the war when I visited Austria, I made a trip to Wiener Neustadt and went to the Apotheke to ask whether they still made the cream my mother used. It had been years since she died, and I had a longing for that smell—I still often have that fragrance in my mind when I think of her.)

Our family was modern Orthodox for the time. I have only the vaguest memory of attending Temple—where women were confined to the upper level, seated behind a screen in the traditional manner. But I do recall my feelings of alarm about the *Mikweh*, the ritual bathing performed by Orthodox women after their periods.

My mother, Agnes Bauer,
age thirty.

I didn't have to bathe, of course, but I was taken along by a young girl who watched out for me while my mother went in. I was unreasonably scared by the sound of running water and the mysterious bathing process that regularly absorbed my mother's attention every month. I think it gave me my fear of water. I never became a real ocean or water lover.

CHAPTER 2

Eviction and Prison

DURING THOSE YEARS GROWING UP IN WIENER Neustadt, things were happening in Germany, Austria, and the rest of the world that could not possibly have been understood by a six-year-old girl. I am grateful, now, to have in hand a courageous book titled *Reluctant Return: A Survivor's Journey to an Austrian Town*, written by David W. Weiss, a former professor of immunology at Hebrew University in Israel, and the son of Wiener Neustadt's rabbi, Henrich Hillel Weiss. David's account focuses on his return to Wiener Neustadt in 1995, when he visited the site of the Temple and the remains of the Jewish cemetery. The last time he had been there was 1938, shortly after Austria joined the Third Reich and the Jews were expelled from the city. Prompted by his reuniting with the other few Jewish survivors of the congregation Kehillah Kedoshah Wiener Neustadt, David provides important details about Wiener Neustadt and its now-vanished Jewish community.

The Temple congregation in 1938 numbered more than one thousand. All were aware of the growth of the Nazi Party, which had its adherents in Austria as well as Germany, and they watched with growing alarm as Austrian chancellor Kurt von Schuschnigg began negotiating with Hitler over the prospect of an *Anschluss*— an agreement to unite Germany with Austria. For a time, it seemed as if Schuschnigg would be successful in resisting this measure, but at a crucial point in the negotiations, Schuschnigg folded, resigning his post, and ordered Austrian troops not to resist the Germans. On March 12, 1938, Hitler and his troops rode into Vienna, and Austria was annexed on March 13.

In Max's words: "The street of the little provincial town in which we live is full of Nazi flags—not one single window that doesn't show the flag—except ours. Jews are not allowed to show the symbols of the 'Reich.' Everybody stares at our flagless windows. First sign of discrimination appears: behavior of teacher and students at school is changing. I am the only one who is not allowed to raise his hand for the Hitler salute. My uncle's store and all other Jewish establishments in the city are marked with a poster: 'Jewish Store—Don't Buy.' "

• • • • •

Shortly after the annexation, Jews were congregated to the inner city of Wiener Neustadt. Families had to share apartments. That was when we were forced to leave our second-floor apartment, the one with the cozy kitchen where I had spent so many nap-time hours.

As Max recalled, "We were expelled from our apartment; a Nazi neighbor denounced us as not being worthy to share the neighborhood with her, and we were forced to move and share an apartment with another Jewish family." We were placed in an apartment on the

Wiener Strasse, very close to the Jewish Temple. (My parents parti-
tioned off our part of the apartment to give us some privacy.) Lilly
and I did not understand at all what was going on, and I only have
a blurred memory of the quarters we shared with that other family.

We could not have been there very long.

On November 10, 1938, came Kristallnacht. All through
Germany and many parts of Austria, storm troopers and civilians ransacked and burned Jewish synagogues and businesses.
Our Temple in Wiener Neustadt was a two-story building built
of carved stone, with stately arched windows, crenellated balus-
trades along the roofline, and a huge, elegant round window
framing the Star of David. On the night of Kristallnacht, it was
pillaged by storm troopers. When the carnage was over, the stone
structure was still standing. (Later, during the war, it would be
entirely demolished.)

As a little girl, I did not understand the gravity of what was happening to Jews throughout Austria and Germany until the day
when—like so many others—we received the knock on the door.
Perhaps someone had denounced us again. Or maybe the men in
black boots simply went door to door, driving out Jews from all the
apartments near the Temple. I don't know. I didn't recognize the
men who appeared at our door, or know why they came, or understand what they said. I only knew we had to leave again—all of us,
my father, my brother, my sister, and me. The apartment and everything in it no longer belonged to us or the other family living there
as well.

All our possessions had to stay—our furniture, clothing, paintings, jewelry, and toys. Mama was only permitted to carry a small

bag with a few necessary items. The doors were locked behind us, the keys taken by the men in the black boots.

In the turmoil that followed, my father and brother vanished. They had been taken away by those men. I didn't know where. My mother, carrying one small bundle under her arm, led Lilly and me through the streets to the Temple.

Though I didn't absorb how much destruction had occurred within our synagogue, I could see that it was no longer the same place where we had worshipped. The floor was covered with mounds of straw. This is where we would sleep.

Mama had grown up on a farm. Compared to many others who had spent their entire lives in Wiener Neustadt, she was relatively used to simple quarters and knew how to make the best of the situation. But I wondered what this was like for other members of the congregation, those who were used to sleeping on fine linens in canopied beds. Mama, Lilly, and I tried to manage and make ourselves reasonably comfortable in the straw bedding. But what about those city people from elegant homes who, presumably, had never experienced a single moment of discomfort in their lives? We knew a number of these families.

• • • • •

After several nights in the Temple, we were forced to move again. As we were marched through the streets alongside other Jewish people from the Temple, we passed empty storefronts of silent shops scrawled with swastikas and anti-Semitic slogans. Jeering boys surrounded us, pelting us with rocks and shrieking *"Juden! Juden!"* My mother tried to protect us, but there was no mistaking the danger that we were in. A horrifying change had taken place in Wiener Neustadt.

Our destination, the jailhouse called *Kreisgericht,* was the county jail of Wiener Neustadt. Perhaps fifty women and children were crammed into one cell. There were no men, and since our eviction from the apartment, we had heard no news about my father and brother. I'm sure there were hushed consultations among the women, and terrible reports and rumors, but I don't recall anything being explained to Lilly and me. We could only follow and observe. Nothing we saw made any sense.

Then . . . I turned red. To this day I don't know what it was that caused me to break out with red blotchy patches all over my body. But those around me, including my mother, immediately imagined the worst. The symptoms suggested scarlet fever, a highly contagious, deadly streptococcus infection. Without antibiotics, scarlet fever was often fatal. Even the guards must have been alarmed by the sight of me, for they immediately called the prison doctor.

The doctor ordered that my mother and I should be isolated in a separate cell. Eight-year-old Lilly begged to go with us, but they wouldn't let her. She became hysterical, clawing at the jail window bars, screaming, "I want out! I want out!"

This was the worst—to be torn away from my sister. I could still hear Lilly's screams after Mama and I were escorted to our isolated cell.

I cannot begin to imagine what Mama was feeling at that moment. What can a mother feel being jailed with one child, the other one desperate, beyond reach, and a husband and son who have disappeared without a trace?

I have an indelible memory of her reaction and its impact on me. She crumpled into a chair, covered her face with both hands, and started to cry. It was the first time I had seen her cry. I was terrified. Here was my protector and life security, crying. *Mothers don't cry*, I thought.

I caressed her face with my hands and said "Mama please don't cry, everything will be good." I felt totally helpless. When would someone come to our rescue?

It was one of the worst experiences I had as a child.

· · · · ·

With Lilly's desperate shrieks still ringing in my ears—and the sight of her clawing at the bars—I thought she must be as inconsolable as Mama. But fortunately she was not entirely among strangers. Frau Buchsbaum, our seamstress and friend, was also in that cell with part of her family. She must have taken Lilly under her wing. I'm sure other mothers also did their best to comfort Lilly and assure her that we would be reunited.

As for my suspicious red body, it was established by the doctor that it was only a rash, perhaps caused by something in the cell. What is more likely is that the blotches were an emotional reaction caused by fear. In any case, the rash faded and my skin resumed its normal color. To our dismay, though, Mama and I were kept separate from the others just in case I carried some other communicable infection.

Meanwhile, we had no idea what had become of my father and brother. My mother, I'm sure, feared the worst.

•••••

Though no one told Mama how long we would be held in jail, she must have realized that we would never return to our apartment. For the moment, it seemed safer behind bars than being on the streets where the jeering crowds threw stones and taunted us.

As for that prison time—however long it was—what comes back to me now was the strange, unpleasant taste of the farina we were given every day. Back home, in the comfort of my mother's kitchen, our daily serving of farina was comforting. It was what we called the *Zehn Uhr Jause,* a small meal occurring regularly at ten o'clock every morning, midway between our breakfast and lunch. That farina, the kind I had grown up on, was wonderfully tasty, served with hot milk, sugar, and cinnamon. Not the farina in prison. The stuff we were served every morning for breakfast was wretched tasting—watery and salty. But I swallowed it with closed eyes. It was either that, or go hungry.

•••••

Inexplicably, we were on the move again. It was night, and there were buses waiting. As the cells emptied out, we were finally rejoined by Lilly, who clung to us as if she would never let go. Guards ushered us outside to board the buses.

And then, seeming to appear from nowhere, there was my father—and Max! It was an ecstatic reunion. Even though none of us knew where we were going, or what would happen next, it felt as if, finally, there was hope for our future. Now that all of us were together again, perhaps things would not be so bad after all.

But my father was not the same. Was it on that bus ride that I noticed how he had changed—or only later, in Vienna, when we were again living together as a family? All the warmth and energy seemed to have drained out of him. Once so protective of us, especially when our mother was in high dudgeon, he now seemed remote, almost indifferent, and very silent. As for what he had experienced in the hands of the storm troopers, he never spoke a word to his children. I believe that my mother, too, was never told. Josef Bauer was still alive, but some essential part of my father had vanished into the darkness.

What exactly happened to him I can only imagine. From the visible change in my father, I assume he was beaten, probably tortured, but this was not something that would be told to his six- and eight-year-old daughters. Max would have told me in later years if he had known. But when he and my father were taken, the men were separated from the boys, and Max did not witness what my father had to endure.

Whatever occurred, the man on the bus with us was not the same man. He was no longer the father I had known.

CHAPTER 3

Transported to Vienna

MY FAMILY WAS ALL TOGETHER AGAIN! THAT IS WHAT I remember best about that bus ride from Wiener Neustadt. In my six-year-old mind and heart, nothing could go wrong. Father, Mother, brother Max, sister Lilly, and I were all reunited.

I was completely happy. The fact that we were crowded onto a dark bus, carrying nothing but the bundle my mother had under her arm, traveling to an unknown destination through the depths of the night, held no threat for me. All would be well, now that we had found one another.

This photograph of me, taken in 1939 when I was six, was used on my Nazi identification card.

I had no way of knowing that this was the beginning of a massive Nazi Party effort to purge Jews from every part of Austria and forcibly herd them into a single district in Vienna. The Second *Bezirk* (Second District), called Leopoldstadt, was to be our destination—and that of thousands of other Jews from all of Austria. (This area is actually an island lying between the Danube River that curves around to the north and the Danube Canal cutting across the bend in the river.)

Although I didn't know it at the time, Jews from the outer districts of Vienna were also being moved into the Leopoldstadt, where they would be forced to share apartments with families already living there. Of course, no one had made any provision for the sudden influx. Each family had to fend for itself—upon arrival, they were instructed simply "to disappear." They were told, "Jews get lost," and no one hesitated.

We were among the few families fortunate enough to have relatives living in Vienna. Miraculously, upon our arrival, we were greeted by my father's oldest brother, my Uncle Bernhard. I have no idea how the message got through to him that we were on our way to Vienna. Perhaps he just assumed we had to be on one of the buses descending on the city. Or perhaps my family was able to send word to him. In any case, we looked upon him as our rescuer, which indeed he was.

Uncle Bernhard, Vienna, 1938.

Uncle Bernhard mostly wore a black vest buttoned all the way up his chest, a soft dark jacket with rounded lapels, and a high-collar white shirt fronted with a stylishly elegant bow tie. I don't think I ever saw him when he wasn't in a suit of this kind.

My uncle took us to his apartment home. We were welcomed with open arms by my Aunt Sarah, even though, as we could readily see, the large apartment was becoming crowded. Uncle Bernhard had already taken in my cousins and their families who had been forced to leave their own apartments in other districts of Vienna. Despite that, to me the apartment seemed spacious and luxurious, especially since I had recently been sleeping on straw and on prison mattresses. Now I found myself in a real, soft bed, enjoying the luxury of sleeping between clean sheets, just as I had before we were arrested. As if by magic, we were living in heated, beautifully furnished rooms with running water, getting delicious meals, surrounded by family.

Since my father was the youngest in his family of eight children and therefore among the last to marry, most of the cousins of my own generation were considerably older than I was. Among my favorites (due to remain so all my life) was his daughter Else, who was then in her early thirties. She was so outgoing, warm, and affectionate that from the moment I first met her I felt as if she had adopted me.

Cousin Else was, and would always remain, a role model in my life. She was dark-haired, slender, attractive, very chatty, and very understanding, no matter what the circumstances. In time I would come to realize this warmhearted cousin was also very liberal in her thinking. As for Else's husband, Martin Jahoda, I could not have known very much about him at the time. But later on I would find out that he was regarded as an influential intellectual who, with a partner, established the prestigious printing firm of Profil Druck (Profile Press).

Another older cousin was also present in the household. This was Bertha. She wore glasses and had a squeaky voice. When I compared her to her sister Else or to my own mother (which I inevitably did), Bertha always seemed to me a bit sluggish and helpless. But she, like Else, was a very warm presence, and paid much attention to us kids.

Lilly and I were at the age where we doted on small children. We adored Bertha's son, little Eric, who was always beautifully dressed. He wore the kind of velvet suit, high collar, and soft tie worn by Austrian toddlers in those days. To Lilly and I, Eric could do no wrong.

Uncle Bernhard, however, was unimpressed by the cuteness of small children. He maintained the demeanor of a strict disciplinarian, and I vividly remember how he corrected Eric right in front of us. When Eric spoke out of turn, he was told by his grandfather that he would "have to go, turn around, and stand in the corner." Lilly and I felt sorry for Eric: his infractions, whatever they were, seemed very small. But a command from Uncle Bernhard could not to be disobeyed. I, too, was intimidated by my uncle, and did my best trying to help both of us stay on his good side, which meant keeping out of his way.

Could my family have stayed on with Uncle Bernhard? It seems likely he would have sheltered us as long as we needed a place to stay, but my mother was determined for us to find our own place. I think she regarded her three young children as rowdy noisemakers in that sedate home, and she must have felt that remaining with my uncle would be an intolerable imposition. Also, by the time we moved in, the household already had far more than its usual number of people.

CHAPTER 4

Herminengasse 15

MAMA SOON BEGAN COMBING THE STREETS OF the Second District searching for a place where our family could be living by ourselves and not have to share with another family. While Christians were also living in this district, it was the only part of Vienna where Jews were assigned to live. If we were going to have a more permanent home, it was there she would have to look.

What Mama discovered, with the help of Uncle Bernhard, was a ground-floor set of rooms adjacent to a deserted store. It may have been a store left empty by Jewish owners when they were forced to close and most likely emigrate. The location, Herminengasse 15, seemed barely adaptable to the needs of a small family, but my mother found just the degree of privacy and security she was seeking. It was this apartment that would be our home for the next seven years. We were now living in the midst of the Jewish ghetto of Vienna.

These are Max's memories of that time: "Father's health was constantly getting worse. We live without any plans for the future, just from day to day like all the other Jewish people too, three and four families living in overcrowded apartments or in abandoned stores transformed into habitations, like ours."

Max in front of our building, Herminengasse 15.
Our apartment is just to the left of where he is
standing.

The old building, probably dating from the nineteenth century, still had features that seemed almost medieval. Across the storefront of the apartment were heavy, metal folding doors and iron bars that fell into place to keep the doors permanently locked. What had once been the store was nothing more than an uninhabitable loft, a dingy room with oily floors. Just off the store-front area, accessed through a side door, was a pair of rooms that must have once served as a storage area.

In these two rooms my mother improvised living quarters for the five of us. The front room, entered from the dark lobby of the building, she converted into a kitchen. It had a portable petroleum stove with two burners that could be used for some cooking and a coal-fired *herd*, or stove, that served to provide heat but could also be used for cooking. There was a bed nearby the *herd* in the kitchen, and I recall this as being the place where my father slept after we first moved in. We also had a kitchen table that could seat our family.

We had no electricity in this apartment. When it got dark, we lit one petroleum lamp. In cold months a second, small coal-fired stove in the one living room/bedroom provided heat. In summer, my mother used the small, petroleum-fired, two-burner cooker so she could prepare meals without heating up the whole kitchen.

Against one wall of the kitchen was an iron sink flanked with decorative etchings. The only toilet, located in a walled-in cubicle in one corner of the kitchen, had an overhead tank and a pull-string for flushing.

There was no separate bathroom, and we had just one faucet located over the kitchen sink. When it was time to do the dishes, Mama would heat up some water and put it in a large bowl. For washing up, we pulled out another metal bowl called a *lavoir*, heated up more water, poured it into the bowl, and washed, one at a time.

(Later, during the war, we got into the routine of making monthly visits to the public Turkish baths, the *Roemerbad*. An exotic-looking place with walls covered with cracked mosaics, the *Roemerbad* was old. But even in a state of disrepair, it served our purpose. By going together into the *Roemerbad*, Lilly and I could rent a single bath for the price of one. After paying our entry fee, we were greeted by a "bath lady" who handed us a key, a towel, and soap, then led us to a large room with a huge tub.)

Beyond the kitchen in our apartment, a second room served as bedroom and living quarters. Two old wooden beds stood along one wall, with a cast-iron bed opposite. Max slept in one of the wooden beds, Lilly in the cast-iron bed, while my mother and I shared the second wood-frame bed. I was happy to sleep with my mother in one bed. I would cuddle up with her at night, especially in the depths of winter when we did not have the stove burning at night and it was bitter cold.

Though it was not clear to me at the time, I suppose all our furnishings were donated, scavenged, or given to us by relatives, since we had brought nothing from Wiener Neustadt except our meager collection of belongings. Much old furniture had been left behind by the many Jews who emigrated.

Mama did what she could to make the place livable. These projects were undertaken by her alone, as Lilly and I were too young to help and our brother, Max, was considered "not handy." (We used to say, "He was our mind but not our hand.") Mama's inventiveness was admirable. She first painted the kitchen white just to cover up the dirt, but when that did not satisfy her, she got some blue paint. She dipped the brush into the blue paint, and sweeping her arm back and forth, splashed the paint on the wall creating a dappled effect. (I would call this today the "Jackson Pollock look.") At first, we were shocked by what my mother had done, but after living with it a while, we had to admit it did not look too bad. The pattern of blue speckles on a white background really did give the kitchen a more cheerful appearance.

• • • • •

The privacy of that apartment was one of its most attractive features. One door led from the "living room" of the apartment into a small, enclosed courtyard, separated by a stone wall from the neighboring building's courtyard. The privacy afforded by this entryway was very important to us, as Lilly and I could go out there and quietly catch some fresh air. (Later, when Vienna was bombed, we would fetch wood blocks from ruined buildings and bring them back to the little courtyard and saw them into usable sizes for our stove.) True, nosy neighbors could look down on us from above, so Mama was constantly shushing us to make sure we didn't draw the ire of unsympathetic residents. But she felt it was far safer for us to play in the small courtyard rather than public areas.

The building had one other feature that, later on, would play a crucial role in concealing my family from prying eyes. From the back of the lobby of the building, a door led directly into the courtyard. To the right of this passageway was an area where some residents kept their bicycles and garbage pails. To the left were stairs going down to the cellar where residents had small cubicles mostly used for their supplies of coal and wood. My mother or brother would descend the cellar stairs carrying a small shovel, returning with a pail of coal. I rarely went down. It was unthinkable that such a dark, cramped space could be inhabited by anyone—much less most of the families in the building. I had no way of knowing that, in future, that cellar would be the means of our survival during the last week before liberation.

CHAPTER 5

Deportation and Death

I N RECOUNTING THE BEGINNINGS OF OUR NEW LIFE on Herminengasse, I realize I have said little about my father. The change I have described seemed to be permanent, and there was no time when I can remember him behaving like the father I had known before those ugly days in Wiener Neustadt when he was separated from us.

Papa was a nonstop smoker. I can still see him in those months after we moved into the Vienna apartment, occupying most of his days quietly rolling his own cigarettes. He would open a package of papers, take out a single sheet that he held poised in one hand, distribute a dribbling of tobacco along the length of the paper, lick the edge, and roll it closed. There was the flare of a match, the faint odor of sulfur. He smoked as if it absorbed all his attention.

I can only imagine what it was like for my mother to be living with and caring for a husband who was a ghost of his former self. The handsome, dashing partner of her youth—the man who dressed impeccably, who raced motorcycles and made friends instantly— was gone, replaced by someone whose spirit was broken. Though I didn't know why, I was aware that I could no longer count on him to intercede when my mother was angry—or, indeed, ever respond as he once had. He seemed to have gone into a steep decline. Some seven months after we moved into our lodgings in Herminengasse, my father was taken to the hospital.

Sometime afterward, I recall Max and my mother standing in the kitchen, both well dressed in dark clothing. They may have come from the hospital or even the funeral. Lilly and I were not told exactly what had happened to our father.

Immediately after we learned of my father's death, I recall some behavior of my own that, to this day, I cannot quite explain. For some reason it seemed important that I announce to the world that my father had passed away, but the means I took to make the announcement seems bizarre to me now. Among my most cherished possessions was an old doll carriage that had just three wheels. Though it teetered precariously as I pushed it around, I must have felt very important trundling it along the street outside our building. Soon after hearing the news from my mother and Max, I got out the carriage and steered it out the front door. Looking up at passing strangers, I announced, "My father died! My father died!"

I'm sure it was only a child's confused way of dealing with something she could not possibly understand. It was unfathomable the way my father had changed and then passed out of my young life. I do not remember any sorrow or, indeed, anything else at all about the circumstances of his death. Just that image—of a confused, skinny little girl pushing her doll carriage through the streets of the Second District of Vienna, announcing, "My father died!"

Max at age fifteen.
This photo appeared on
his identification card.

It was July 1939. Now, we were a family of four. Somehow we would have to get along without my father. Great responsibility, my mother made clear, now fell upon Max, my brother. Remarkably enough, even at age fifteen, he seemed capable of taking on his newly appointed role. In the next few years, leading up to and during the war, he would indeed be a mainstay and provider as we shaped our daily lives around the dual need to survive as a family and remain invisible to the eyes of authorities. As Max describes things during this time, "I take now and then occasional jobs to earn some small money, moving people's furniture when they move from one crowded apartment to another, even more crowded apartment!"

• • • • •

At the time of my father's death, the apartment house that we lived in was packed with Jewish families living two or three to an apartment.

One family we got to know very well was that of Frau Sidie and her partner, Herr Fritz, who occupied a third-floor apartment with their son, Willie (and, not least of all, Willie's cute little fox terrier, named Chippie). Everyone seemed to know that Frau Sidie was not married to Herr Fritz, but Herr Fritz seemed to live with them. Herr Fritz was a tall man, a little on the heavy side, but attractive. I learned that he was married to another woman who also lived in Vienna, and in that "other" family he had several grown children.

Frau Sidie was a beautiful blue-eyed blond lady with a warm, comforting manner who could win your friendship immediately. (In the years to come, she would become a hero in my eyes—a courageous woman who, more than once, risked her own life to save others.)

Their son, Willie, was a very handsome young man just three years older than Lilly. Before long, Lilly was making regular visits to the family's third-floor apartment. Ostensibly, Lilly went up to help Frau Sidie in the kitchen, but it soon became clear that my sister was interested in more than housework. People smiled when they talked of "Willie and Lilly." I believe it was her first romance.

Another person who would play an important role in our lives in Herminengasse 15 was our building's superintendent, Herr Vicecka. His background was Czech, and like most Czechs he was no friend of Hitler. Liquor was important to Mr. Vicecka. He was in the habit of spending his evenings at the corner *Gasthaus* (wine bar) and was quite happy when he could have his glass of wine (mostly, more than one). He was not married as far as we knew but he always had a woman by his side.

Herr Vicecka often wobbled from his carpentry shop on our street to his job as a superintendent in our building, appearing drunk and nearly oblivious to what was going on. After the death of my father, Herr Vicecka took it into his head that he could woo my mother. He must have been dismayed that she never showed the slightest interest—but, as I would later learn, it did not mean my mother was totally resistant to male admirers.

•••••

I now know that the SS and police officials began deporting Jews from Vienna—as well as the rest of Austria—on a large scale beginning in 1939 and continuing through 1943. Most deportations took place between the years of 1941 and 1943. Also the law of forcing Jews to wear the yellow Star of David comes into effect.

Like all the others we also received notification to report to the Palais Rothschild, a stately Jewish family palace that had been usurped by the Nazis and turned into Gestapo headquarters. Our struggle to survive seemed to have come to an end. We were to present ourselves to the "examination board." On the appointed day, we stood on a line with hundreds of others that stretched around the block, waiting to be examined and questioned. It was here where Jews would be ordered to report to a certain deportation train on such and such date.

We finally stood before the examiner, and Mama presented our documents. Then came the decisive moment: the Gestapo official took a few minutes to go through the documents and handed them back to us. He already seemed to know our history as he said quickly, "You are by Nuremberg Laws half-Jews, and will not be deported." The feeling of relief that rushed through our bodies showed on our faces. But could we trust the words of this Gestapo officer? For now, we could only hope so.

· · · · ·

The families in Herminengasse 15 were aware of what was occurring throughout the city—mainly in our district—and they must have realized it would only be a matter of time before the Jewish families in the building would be forcibly rounded up and transported.

While Lilly and I did not totally understand the situation, it was no secret to us that we were in grave danger. Other residents of the building, however, must have decided that our family was the least likely to be deported. It was mostly because we did not wear the yellow Star of David. Perhaps they surmised that since my Jewish father had died and my mother had been born gentile, we had the best chance of escaping deportation. Two residents brought some of their most valuable possessions to us for safekeeping.

The first was Frau Tlumac, a very elegant lady in her seventies who lived upstairs. She brought jewelry to my mother. Her request was simple: "Frau Bauer, can you please try to keep this for me? If I don't come back, use it for your girls." My mother was hesitant as she was not sure what would happen to us. But she still agreed to hold it for safekeeping.

Another neighbor, Frau Tauber, had a crate of valuable china brought down. Her request was the same. We had the crate put into the former storage space of our apartment. Frau Tauber had no idea whether or not she would ever return, but she had faith that my mother would hold it in trust. (I am happy to say that after the war her son, who survived her, was able to pick up the crate with the china.)

•••••

The inevitable finally happened.

Our building was raided in 1942. We were all together in the apartment when the SS or storm troopers came. There was an uproar throughout the building and my mother called out, "They're here! Stay very quiet." We instantly knew what she meant.

Even though we were told that we would not be deported, we knew many families who were taken away despite being declared "half-Jewish" by the examination board.

We worried that Mama might grow hysterical, but instead, she turned absolutely calm. Often my mother seemed very excitable and high strung, but when it really counted, she had a will of iron. At the critical moment when the raid began, she seemed completely under control. She locked the door and told us, "Be quiet, don't make any noise. If they knock on the door, don't answer." I have no idea why she thought this would help us. After all, if they wanted to get us they could kick in the door in a minute. But we obeyed her without questioning.

We became very still, just listening. There were cries, screams, stamping feet, slamming doors. The clamor seemed to go on and on for hours. Gradually, the noise abated. We kept quiet while hours passed. The building grew deathly quiet. We started to move around and could not understand why nobody had knocked on our door. Was it Mama's shushing us that saved us, or had the Gestapo known exactly who lived in every apartment and their status?

Then there was a voice outside the door.

"Frau Bauer! Frau Bauer!"

It was our superintendent, Herr Vicecka.

Mama carefully opened the door, recognizing Vicecka's voice.

"Frau Bauer, they took them all."

My mother was stunned. "They didn't take us. They left us. They didn't even knock on the door."

The building was silent and we were silent, a sadness overcoming us with the realization that our friends and neighbors were gone. It was at once both sad and frightening as we listened to the eerie silence in the building. *Will they be coming back to get us?* We did not say aloud what was in our minds. None of us slept well that night.

It wasn't until much later that we found out that the Gestapo had examined my mother's family records—going back more than three hundred years—confirming that she was born Catholic. Of all the Jewish families in the building, we were the only one spared.

Herr Vicecka made it his duty to begin searching all the empty apartments, undoubtedly hoping to find any bottles of wine or liquor that had been left behind. On the third floor, he found Frau Sidie's apartment empty. He proceeded with his inspection, opening drawers and cupboards in search of spirits. As he opened one of the closets, Herr Vicecka got the scare of his life. A man jumped out of the closet—a complete stranger. The stranger begged Herr Vicecka not to report him, saying he would leave the premises immediately. In all likelihood, the stranger offered to bribe Herr Vicecka, but it was not in Herr Vicecka's nature to cooperate with the Nazis.

As it turned out, this stranger, the only other survivor of the Gestapo purge in our building, was a Jewish man whom Frau Sidie had been hiding from the authorities. Nobody had suspected anything. We later learned his name—Herr Klein. Frau Sidie had taken the precaution of telling Herr Klein what he was to do in the event she and Willie were arrested, giving him the address of a gentile woman who had agreed to take him in for a certain payment.

Herr Klein was fortunate to have been discovered by Herr Vicecka, whose sympathies were certainly not with the Gestapo. Stunned by his discovery, Herr Vicecka simply stepped aside and allowed Herr Klein to put on a raincoat and leave without a word. This is what Herr Vicecka came to tell my mother. (As we would later discover, Herr Klein followed Frau Sidie's previous instructions, making his way to the new address where the gentile woman took him into hiding as arranged with Frau Sidie.)

Sometime near the end of that terrible day, we heard a dog barking in the street. It was Willie's dog, Chippie. For hours, he was racing nervously back and forth on the block looking for his master.

CHAPTER 6

The People We Knew

A S IT TURNED OUT, CHIPPIE WOULD SOON BE returned to his original family. Of all those who were deported that day, only Frau Sidie and Willie came back to Herminengasse 15 after being trucked away. When Herr Fritz returned from work, he found Frau Sidie and Willie gone. He raced desperately to the Gestapo in an effort to get them out. He showed the pictures of his two sons, from his Aryan wife, who had been drafted into the German Army and were fighting for Hitler's cause. He presented this in a very convincing way "My boys are fighting for your Führer. Let this woman and the boy go. Look, does this woman even look Jewish, with her blue eyes and blond hair?" Miraculously, it resulted in the release of Herr Fritz's "second family" and within several days the family returned to our building, much to our delight.

The empty apartments quickly filled with new residents. During the years that followed, while the war continued, I would come to know most of the inhabitants of our building.

It was a polyglot assortment, mainly of couples or families of mixed Jewish religion but also some full Christian (Aryan) families who were given the apartments. Crowded in the same third-floor apartment with Herr Fritz, Frau Sidie, and Willie was the family Hecht. Frau Hecht was gentile, her husband Jewish. They had one daughter, Erna, and for a time everyone wondered whether Erna would win Willie's attention. But his affections never strayed from Lilly despite the closer proximity of Erna.

Living below was a couple in their mid-fifties, Herr and Frau Bruckner. They had no children. Like the Hechts, the Bruckners were mixed religion—Herr Bruckner Jewish and Frau Bruckner gentile. Frau Bruckner was tall, very thin and angular, with graying hair. Her husband was shorter, walked with a cane, and he was totally deaf. Whenever he went out, Herr Bruckner was nattily dressed in suit and tie. At the time I wondered how Frau Bruckner managed to communicate with her husband: it's likely that, through long association, he learned lip reading, at least enough to understand what his wife was trying to tell him.

One frequent visitor to the courtyard just outside our ground-floor apartment was Frau Bergman, a woman in her mid-sixties who had moved onto the fourth floor, which was the top floor in the building. (Above that floor was a bright, sunny attic that was used for drying the wash.) Frau Bergman seemed elderly and mysterious to us, and we wondered why she always trembled. (In all probability she suffered from Parkinson's disease.) She was sort of a recluse, but had a great love for cats, and ultimately it was her affection for them that drew her out of her apartment. Each day, usually around lunchtime, she made her way down the stairs from the top floor with a bowl of prepared food that she placed on top of the head-high courtyard wall. My sister and I peeked from our room in wonder as a herd of feral cats, as if on cue, came leaping over the top of the wall to feast on Frau Bergman's daily offerings. Frau Bergman would stay with the cats, looking on until they finished their meal. Occasionally she intervened with their feeding, pushing one cat or another out of the way to make sure each had a fair share.

Next door to us was the family Churan—again, a mixed-religion couple, the husband gentile, the wife Jewish—with their two young children, Helli and Karli, Jr. Later on, as the years and the war continued, we shared a secret with this family. We would all gather in the Churans' apartment and secretly listen to foreign-radio broadcasts that came in from the BBC, a practice forbidden by the Nazis. (All Jews had to hand in their radios. We were not allowed to own such equipment, but the Churans managed to conceal that radio.) I later surmised that our superintendent, Herr Vicecka, had known all along about the radio, as his apartment shared a common wall with the Churans'. He must have heard the radio but just like he kept the hiding of Herr Klein to himself, he would not go and inform on us.

Max noted in his memoir some of the news we heard: "Denmark and Norway, Holland, Belgium, Luxembourg overrun. France capitulates! Our mood is down. The future looks somber for the Jewish people in Vienna, with Hitler dominating the whole of Europe. . . . But England has not succumbed—that's where new hope is based and the rumor wave again starts to roll. . . . Hitler has still not won the war!"

• • • • •

Of all the families in the building, only one could be counted as Nazi sympathizers. Herr and Frau Kopica were the "Aryan type" that Hitler favored. Herr Kopica had served in the German army and been wounded. He was home, living off his war pension. Hitler encouraged couples like the Kopicas to have many children, and Frau Kopica seemed to be perpetually pregnant. A tall, dark-haired woman, she was missing a couple of teeth, and whenever I saw her, she was wearing a flower-patterned house dress and a plain apron. Though she seemed unattractive to me, we admired the cuteness of her three children—daughters Ditta and Isa (short for Isabella), and a little boy, Franzi, Jr.

Though we often played with the children or took them for walks, we felt we had to be cautious around the Kopicas. They were part of a large family, relatives often visited, and their apartment many times seemed to be full of people. Among their frequent visitors were brothers in SS uniforms and grown, pretty sisters accompanied by uniformed boyfriends. Since my mother did not try to prevent Lilly and me from playing with the Kopica children, my guess is that she thought it good policy to have them as our friends, and perhaps sensed that Frau Kopica was quite glad to have us take the children off her hands from time to time. (As it turned out, this family would be instrumental in saving the lives of most of the Jewish people still left in our building when we were all in the cellar, in the last days before liberation.)

On one occasion Lilly and I had a harrowing experience with these children. In summer my sister and I liked to take Ditta and Isa to the Danube River. It was only ten minutes away from home, and Frau Kopica never had any objections: she was happy to be freed up to do her household chores. The Kopica girls obviously loved being with us. A trip to the Danube was a special occasion, and when we splashed around in the water, they never showed any fear.

Neither Lilly nor I knew how to swim, and normally we stayed in shallow water near the shore. But the banks of the Danube drop off quickly, as we learned to our grief that day. I had taken Isa by her hand while Lilly looked after Ditta. Suddenly, Isa's hand slipped out of my grasp. She started to swim away. I tried to wade after her. In an instant, I was in water up to my chin. At that moment Lilly saw that Isa had begun thrashing. She was drowning—just beyond my reach. Fortunately, Lilly, being taller than I, was able to jump out into the deeper water and pull Isa out before she floated downriver.

As the little girl gasped for air, several witnesses on shore rushed to help us. One of the bystanders took over and pressed the water out of Isa's stomach. The girl recovered quickly; I do not think she even knew what had happened.

But I could never forget that moment. We were terrified. My first thought was, *She almost drowned.* What would happen if we could not save her—this little Aryan girl from a family where all the men were in the army and the SS? What would happen if they found out? *We might disappear like the others.*

At the time, Ditta was about five years old, Isa about three. I don't know whether they even told their parents about the incident. Isa probably did not remember anything about what happened to her, and I suspect that Ditta was too scared to tell because she thought her mother would not let her play with us again. Or, it could be, they told some version of the story but Frau Kopica was not listening to the children's babble.

Lilly and I were so relieved that the kids were returned to their home in one piece that we never even told our mother about it. She would have had sleepless nights for weeks. We both had a bad scare and we never again took them to the Danube River because we feared they would remember what happened there. After all, Lilly and I were just children ourselves. How could we have assumed such responsibility?

CHAPTER 7

The Family in Hiding

IDOLIZED MY OLDER BROTHER—AND STILL DO. I HAD
every reason to do so. From our first arrival in Vienna to the last
days of the war and afterward, what he and my mother accomplished
to ensure our survival was nothing less than a miracle.

Though we were one family in name, one of Hitler's many
monstrous racial edicts divided us in two, placing my mother and
Max on one side and my sister Lilly and I on the other. The divid-
ing line was the *Stichtag*, or cut-off day, a date arbitrarily chosen by
the Nazis to draw the line between "full Jews" and those who were
considered "mixture first degree" *(Mischling Ersten Grades).* Since
my mother had been born Catholic, my father Jewish, and Max
was born before the *Stichtag*, he was considered *Mischling Ersten
Grades.* He did not have to wear the yellow star and he was also
allowed to do designated work. He was, ironically, at one point
called for military mustering. However, once his *Mischling Ersten
Grades* status was discovered, he was declared, as a half-Jew, unfit
to serve in the German army. This was one of the rare bits of good
news our family could enjoy!

But Lilly and I, born after the *Stichtag*, were declared "full Jews" and therefore were supposed to wear the yellow star and were not allowed to attend school. The implications of this were horrendous—exactly what my mother most feared. If any of the authorities identified her daughters as full Jews, Lilly and I might be taken from her and deported.

Faced with this terrifying possibility, living in a district where many of our Nazi-friendly neighbors could be sympathizers, my mother impressed on us that my sister and I must do everything possible to conceal our Jewish identities. This meant that, above all, we must not wear the yellow Jewish star that had been forced upon all Jews. Max did not have to wear it as *Mischling* first degree, but Lilly and I did.

Any move by the authorities that singled us out as Jews was dangerous. There was a frightening moment early in the War when ration cards were issued. All residents of Vienna received them, but for Jews, there was a "J" signifying "Juden" printed on the cards. Every ration sheet contained small stamps, and each stamp also carried the letter "J." Mother's and Max's ration cards were without the "J." But if the cards issued for Lilly and me carried the "J," it would be obvious to the authorities that Mother's daughters were Jews and people around us would consider the whole family Jewish. This would be quickly discovered if we presented the "J"-stamped cards in our neighborhood grocery stores. It was a small community, and we patronized the same stores all the time. Most gentiles living around us did not know anything about a "*Stichtag*," or that we were Jewish.

It was Max who rescued us, and he did it through his connection with Robert Segen. Robert was a close friend whose family, like ours, had been transplanted from Wiener Neustadt to Vienna.

Max describes his friendship with the Segens: "My life is running slow—no school, no job, no future . . . but somehow we are feeling protected against any bad surprise: a Jewish lawyer gives us advice—how to behave in order to avoid trouble with the authorities. This man—our 'protector'—is licensed to defend Jews only. He has already helped many persecuted Jews escape from the Gestapo, especially the rich ones—one must remember that this is a time of giving and taking, different times with different moral concepts—the important thing is to survive! This protector is a family friend since my father's time and we were brought up in the same town. His son is a friend and also an opera fan."

In Vienna, Max and Robert renewed their friendship and Max visited Robert often. The Segens lived in a substantial apartment in a prestigious Vienna district, which was possible because Robert's father, though originally Jewish, had converted to Catholicism when he married a confirmed Catholic woman. (Robert was raised Catholic.) The Segens promoted Robert's and Max's friendship: they adored my brother and really took him under their wing.

Robert's father was a lawyer. I'm not certain what his post was, but he seemed to have strong connections with the proper authorities during the war. (We never knew the identity of Robert's father's close contacts, but they must have been men with considerable influence.) As the desperation and worry of my mother got worse—fearing, every day, what would happen to her two girls—Max approached Dr. Segen and asked for advice on the situation regarding the ration cards. With the family split—we two girls

Jewish and Max registered as *Mischling Ersten Grades*—what should we do? Some uneasy time passed before Dr. Segen returned with his message: we should not wear the yellow Jewish star or use the "J"-stamped food cards until we heard from him. Soon after this discussion Lilly and I received our new ration cards without the "J" stamp. No questions were asked about how this happened. I have no doubt that with this dangerous "procedure" Dr. Segen, our protector, might have saved our lives and probably the lives of others.

Our protector had further advice for my mother. While Lilly and I could only escape detection by not wearing the six-pointed yellow Jewish star, he pointed out that we had to be prepared in the event that our home was inspected by authorities. Mother was to sew the stars on some of the clothing belonging to Lilly and me that always hung in our closet. That way, there would always be a yellow star on our clothing in case an inspection came to the house. These vital instructions were relayed through Max, as was all urgent communication.

The Star of David. This yellow cloth star imprinted with the word "Jude" was sewn onto our clothing that we kept in the closet.

The clothes hanging in our closets, even though out of season, were always ready for inspection. But all of us knew we were taking a chance. If the authorities came to our house, inspected our wardrobe, and found that we had defied regulations, Lilly and I might very well be taken away, or all of us could have been deported. No wonder every knock on the door aroused sheer panic.

• • • • •

Lilly and I knew it was imperative that we take every possible precaution to blend in and not attract any attention. Of the two of us, I was the more likely to be noticed. While Lilly was usually content staying indoors knitting, sewing, or helping Mama with housework, I was more active—a real tomboy—and would go stir-crazy if I couldn't get out and play. Even though I was often outside, however, I felt I was doing a good job of keeping my Jewish identity a secret from the gentile children I played with. One of the games I particularly loved playing with the neighborhood kids was *"Temple Hupfen"* (literally "temple hopper," hopscotch), where we drew square boxes on the asphalt street with a crayon. The object was to hop on one foot only from square to square; if you put your other foot down you were out of the game. We also shot marbles— *"Kugerl Scheiben"*—using holes in the pavement as our targets. All the children I played with were gentile.

Me, age eleven, in Vienna.

One of the neighborhood children I especially liked to play with was Annie. She owned an expensive, fancy *triton*, a scooter, similar to the one my little friend Fritzi owned, but hers was equipped with a foot pedal that made it go terrifically fast. This special conveyance obviously gave her a feeling of superiority, and she exercised a powerful influence over all the children who wanted to try it out. Like the others, I was very tempted to be extra friendly with her, and would do almost anything to get a chance to use her *triton*. But Mama warned me not to get too close to her, and never go to play in her family's apartment. Annie's parents were known to be active party members and might question me. But the temptation to play with Annie was very strong, especially when she actually allowed me to use the *triton* now and then.

It looked like we really could be friends—until the day she pointed at me and called me a "*Juden, Juden, Juden,*" no doubt repeating her parents' words. From then on, I knew I had to avoid any further contact with her, even if it meant never riding her wonderful *triton* again.

CHAPTER 8

The Years Without School

THAT WARINESS, A PERPETUAL SENSE OF IMPENDING danger, the need for caution in our every movement, was a constant in our lives. What we *didn't* do could be as revealing as what we *did* do, which meant that daily role playing was required. Lilly and I, being declared full Jews, were not allowed to go to school. Gentile children of my age went to school during the week: therefore, it had to appear to the neighbors as if I were going to school. At about 7:45 several mornings each week—wearing a school dress and carrying a leather schoolbag on my back as it was custom at the time—I would set out for the streetcar. To all appearances I was just another little Viennese girl on her way to school. What no one knew was my actual destination, which was the home of my mother's second cousin in the 15th District.

Hilda was the daughter of my Aunt Anna, a distant cousin on my mother's side, and she had a new baby, Peter. Hilda understood why I needed to maintain the appearance of going to school, and she was happy to have me babysit for little Peter, pleased that her boy had a playmate. Occasionally, too, I did even more by helping Hilda with light housework.

On the days I "went to school," I would stay with Hilda and Peter until about noon, then take the streetcar back to my neighborhood. I always returned to Herminengasse 15 at a leisurely pace, impressing on anyone who might be watching that I was just another typical schoolchild dawdling on her way home.

Such charades became second nature. I was acutely aware that danger could be lurking behind every glance or comment. One morning when I was in the 15th District pushing Peter in his stroller in a nearby park, I noticed a policeman eyeing me with what seemed like special attention. I felt a jolt of fear. I immediately leapt to the conclusion that he must be thinking *Why isn't this girl in school where she belongs?* As casually as possible, I turned the stroller and headed the other way, my heart pounding. At any moment I expected him to grab me and demand an explanation.

After that, I urged my mother to tell Hilda I could never take Peter outside. The risk was too great.

· · · · ·

Another weekly bit of playacting was required of Lilly and me when our Mother thought it was a good idea for us to show ourselves on some Sunday mornings in the neighborhood church where our nosy neighbors would worship. We put on our best clothes and headed off to the *Karmeliter Kirche*, the neighborhood church. During mass, we simply followed the lead of the congregation when people sat, stood, sang, or kneeled. We made sure some of the people who knew us were aware of our presence in church. But both of us dreaded the part of the service where people went forward to have the priest place wafers on their tongues. That's when Lilly and I always slipped away hoping not to be noticed. Afterward, we laughed in relief at having been successful once again in avoiding this ritual.

· · · · ·

Another mission, and this I performed daily, after my pretend school hours, was taking a hot lunch to Max at his workplace. (As a *Mischling Ersten Grades*, he was allowed to work and was assigned to a factory outfitted for the war effort.) I carried a three-tier tiffin lunchbox with food prepared by my mother. The first stage of the journey was on the underground *(Stadtbahn)* which I took to Pilgrimstrasse station in the 7th District. I made my way to a small factory building and climbed a short flight of stairs to enter the office of the business known as Albert Schoen Galvanisierungsanstalt.

Though the factory was owned by the father, Herr Schoen, management of the office was in the hands of the daughter, Frau Deutsch, a beautiful young woman with a slender figure who always wore lipstick. She wore a blue work coat, unbuttoned in the front, usually over a lovely dress. I was impressed with her, admiring her both for her attractiveness and her friendliness toward Max and me. When I appeared, she would turn and call out "Maxiiiii!" in a voice more sweet than commanding. (Since she spoke to me in much the same way, she never seemed like "a real boss" to me.)

Max came into the office, and I handed him his lunch pail. He was dressed in the blue-jean kind of outfit typical of all the other factory workers, and it always struck me as odd to see my adolescent brother, who I considered an intellectual for his age, dressed for manual labor. It was a quick hello and goodbye. I do not think he ever took a real lunch break. He ate and went right back to work.

This was an errand I never liked since I would only see Max for a minute or two before I had to turn around and retrace my route home. I would have much preferred to spend my entire afternoon playing on the street or in the park near our apartment.

CHAPTER 9

Organisation Tod

MAX CONTINUES WITH HIS STORY:

"A decisive year: I have been notified for military mustering—rejected, of course, as 'half-Jew' and not worthy to serve in the German army . . . but assigned to a manual labor. Luckily and mysteriously I find a comprehensible woman boss who—officially—is a Nazi party member, but inherently opposed to the regime, which I find out quickly. . . . We galvanize the tubes for the cannons of submarines. It's a drab and dull job, but I feel quite safe and make a small weekly salary.

"War with Russia—a terrible shock for the Jews who still hope to emigrate. The last way to escape (via Siberia) to the U.S.A. is now closed; our destiny is sealed: we have to stay in Nazi Vienna. The Germans make spectacular successes on the Eastern Front; the Russians retreat, suffering enormous losses, the war seemingly never to end.

"November: winter comes and stops the German advance—the war will go on. . . ."

• • • • •

Max worked six days a week at the munitions factory managed by Frau Deutsch where I delivered his lunch. Before the war, it had been a galvanizing factory, but like many business owners, Frau Deutsch was forced to become a Party member and convert the factory to support the war effort.

As she would eventually prove to us in the best way possible, Frau Deutsch, as Max explained, had no real sympathy for the Nazis. And she had a very real affection for my brother. I could hear the fondness in her voice whenever I went to deliver Max's lunch—just in the way she would draw out his name, "Maxiiiii," the tone of a mother calling her favorite child in from the playground. Ultimately, she would save his life.

It happened when Maxi was called up to serve in the Organisation Tod, an army corps for draft-age men who were half-Jewish, gypsies, or otherwise regarded as persona non grata by the Nazis. Maxi had no forewarning, and no understanding of what happened to the men sent to the OT. Orders were delivered, saying he must appear for duty. He was to bring a change of underwear, a few pair of socks, nothing more. A deep cloud now hung over our family. Maxi was our protector, the head of the family—we depended on him. How could we do without him? What would happen to him?

Mother tried to pack into his rucksack much more than he was told to bring. It was with a mother's love that she made sure he took along the warmest underwear, the best-repaired socks, and whatever warm clothing he had. We all got up very early in the morning to say our goodbye to Max, not having any idea whether or not he would ever return.

When Maxi had told Frau Deutsch, she immediately understood the implications. Being called up for Organisation Tod was a death sentence. Men entering the OT were sent into combat, but not to fight. They carried no weapons. It was their task to dig ditches and perform other menial tasks that put them directly in the line of fire. To the Nazis, the OT recruits were disposable. When killed, they were simply replaced on the front line by other "undesirables" that became cannon fodder. The ones that held out to the end were then shot by the Nazis. Frau Deutsch knew that if my brother was sent, his name would soon be added to the unending list of fatalities.

Maxi went to the barracks as ordered. Frau Deutsch showed up even before Max arrived. She made sure her party badge was very visible, and had on her usual lipstick—she was beautiful. She acknowledged the officers with a verbal "Heil Hitler!" as well as the right-hand salute, and then proceeded to argue with them. Why did they want to take her best man away from the munitions factory? Did they not realize that her factory was critical to the war effort? Max was her most valuable employee; he was indispensable to her if they wanted to fulfill the armament program of the factory. Without him, production would suffer significantly, as Max was operating a certain machine which required special skill. How could they withdraw such a worker from our munitions factory? Max reported this story to us with amazement, telling us, "At the last minute that 'Nazi' woman, the boss of the factory, saved me." We could hardly believe Frau Deutsch's behavior and incredible courage.

Frau Deutsch prevailed. Maxi's draft orders were canceled. He returned to the factory where he would continue his employment until the end of the war. It was only later, when we learned what happened to OT draftees, that we realized what a close call this was. Once again, Max and our family had been saved. To Frau Deutsch we owed undying gratitude.

CHAPTER 10

Staatsoper—Maxi's Säulensitz Nummer 75

MAX ADORED MY MOTHER. HE DID NOT CALL HER "Mama" or "Mother." He called her "Gold." Sometimes when she was angry for one reason or another, he would grab her around the waist, lift her into the air, and playfully tell her he would not let her down until she would "calm down!"

Clearly, he was a heart stealer. And the way Max found his way into people's hearts was one of the things that helped us survive. My mother knew this. She adored Max as much as he did her. Anything my mother could do for Maxi, she would.

· · · · ·

It was for our mother's sake, as well as Maxi's, that Lilly and I performed the most rigorous of all our missions. Approximately once a month (sometimes twice), either Lilly or I had to rise at five or six in the morning and make our way to the public theater ticket building to try to buy an opera ticket for Max for that day's performance. Opera had taken hold of Max's imagination ever since the days he began listening to gramophone recordings with our cousin Ernoe (the son of our Uncle Wilhelm) in Wiener Neustadt. Now, living in Vienna, Max had an opportunity to hear live opera in one of the greatest opera houses in the world, the Staatsoper of Vienna. Even at the height of the war, the government-sponsored company continued to perform its full repertoire featuring preeminent stars of the opera world. Jews, however—even half-Jews—were not permitted to attend cultural performances. But Max did not have to wear the yellow star, and if he stayed out of trouble and did not attract attention, he was seen as just another opera fan. At any rate, there were so few Jews left in Vienna at the time that it did not occur to anyone to suspect a Jew among them who was not wearing the yellow Star of David.

Max learned to know all the opera stars by their performances, and he familiarized himself with the entirety of musical opera history. The opportunity to attend these performances afforded Max a break from the dull routine of his work, and a distraction from the fear we certainly were all feeling, and helped create a sense of normalcy—or at least the temporary illusion of normalcy.

Since opera was one of the leading cultural events in the city, however, tickets were always in demand. Most performances sold out early on the day tickets went on sale. Our family lived frugally, but Max was the wage earner, and surely he deserved this indulgence. The challenge was to obtain a certain ticket for him which was inexpensive because it was considered a "pillar seat" (*Säulensitz*), one that afforded the spectator only a partial view. *Säulensitz* usually had hardly any view of the performance. Particularly valued, though, was the second-tier *Säulensitz* that offered much more than an obstructed view—it was *Säulensitz Nummer 75*. This prized seat would go quickly, which was why we had to rise early and get to the head of the line if Max were to have a chance at getting the choice seating without an obstructed view. If we could not get a ticket for *Säulensitz Nummer 75*, Max would have to wait until the night of the performance and get a standing-room ticket.

Obtaining this ticket was a demanding task. When it was my turn, Mama would wake me when it was still dark. On cold winter mornings when the fire had been banked all night in the apartment, it was sheer torture climbing out from the warm featherbed. I dressed in haste, splashed a little cold water on my face, took a few bites of bread, and sipped the hot chocolate that Mama prepared for us every morning. Then I hurriedly began to get dressed. First, I had to fuss with the garter belt, which gave me the usual trouble. When I put on the bulky ribbed brown stockings that reached above my knees, I had to attach them to the garter, a slingshot-like apparatus that invariably snapped off at times against my skin. This did nothing for my already tenuous mood at having to awaken so early. I continued with the rest of my clothing, and would bundle up in the brown overcoat that had been made for me by Frau Buchsbaum. (As I had grown, the coat had been let out a couple of times and made longer to reach below my knees.) Then, with whispered cautions from Mama, I headed out through the darkened streets from the Second District over the Augarten Bridge along the Kai on to the Rotenturmstrasse into the Graben and one of the side streets that was the Braeunerstrasse where the ticket bureau was located. By the time I arrived, people were already standing in line, and it was mostly those who wanted to buy less expensive tickets, which sold out first.

The ticket window didn't open until eight o'clock. Time seemed to crawl. There was no opportunity to step out of line—I would lose my place! As the queue grew longer, it became obvious that I was the only child in line. The adults seemed oblivious to my presence.

Many in the crowd knew each other. They were mostly opera fanatics, regulars at the ticket office who entertained themselves with "opera talk," discussing who was in which opera, who sang with a cold, what aria was superb in this or that opera, how one would get a ticket more easily when the Konetzni sisters were singing, etcetera. I was happy they were so busy with their opera talk, which took their attention away from me. Every now and then, though, someone would ask, "Who are you buying tickets for?" and I would answer, very shortly, "For my brother." I tried not to make further conversation and avoided any more questions. I felt I had to be constantly wary and alert. But I think some people felt sorry for this little girl standing in line for opera seats so early in the cold morning.

I stood firmly in line, determined not to lose my place. All the while, with a desperate grip I clutched the precious coins that Mama had given me and prayed that *Säulensitz Nummer 75* would still be available by the time I reached the head of the line.

At long last the ticket window opened. The crowd stirred. I stepped forward to the window. This was the moment of truth. Would Maxi's prized seat with the partially obstructed view still be available?

"*Säulensitz Nummer 75, bitte!*" I said quickly, trying to keep the tremor from my voice. When I was successful, I was ecstatic. (And that number, 75, would remain forever in my head.) The moment Max's ticket was safely in my hand, all the waiting seemed worthwhile. The cold and discomfort seemed to vanish in an instant, and I was overcome with eagerness to rush home and announce the victory.

Rain or shine, this is how we stood in line to get opera tickets for Max. It was a small service to provide, when I think about how much Maxi sacrificed for us.

• • • • •

Max was ebullient after seeing those performances. He kept urging Lilly and me to sing. Lilly refused, but I was an inveterate ham, always happy to burst into song and render my version of a coloratura's high notes. "Go higher! Go higher!" Max would prompt, as I stretched my young vocal cords to the maximum in shrill imitation of a distraught, lovelorn diva.

Mother kept shushing us—as she always did. She feared that a complaint from the neighbors could have consequences.

Needless to say, Max remained dissatisfied with my performances. To him there was no voice more beautiful than that of Erna Sack, the German coloratura soprano. Though Mama always hated to go out in the evening, eventually Max managed to drag her to one of Erna Sack's evening concerts. I don't think my mother was nearly as impressed as Max was. But of course that was understandable. It was impossible to imagine anyone having as much enthusiasm for the opera as my dear brother.

(His love of opera only increased as he grew older. He knew the history of all his favorite opera singers and always kept track of when and where they sang. In later years, after the war, when he could have easily afforded good seats, many times he preferred standing room as it gave him the opportunity to share the performance experience and conversations with young music students. Frugal though he was, throughout his life, when it came to a sold-out performance that Max wanted to see, nothing offered by a ticket scalper was ever too expensive to buy.)

CHAPTER 11

Visas and Partings

ALREADY, IN TELLING MY STORY, I HAVE BLURRED a timeline that extends from our first days in Vienna until the end of the war and shortly after. But it's hard to be specific about events that were occurring during that time. After all, I was only six years old when the family had to move to Vienna. As I have noted, my understanding of world events and the terrible dangers confronting my family and all Jews came filtered through what adults were talking about, what I overheard, and what a little girl experienced in a city gripped by fear and war. That is the reason I have included excerpts from Max's notes throughout my story, as he was very aware of the political climate at the time and followed it closely.

But we all lived in a constant state of alertness and fear. By the time we moved to Vienna, I had seen my family evicted twice from our home. I had slept on straw on a Temple floor, been thrown in jail, separated from my sister, brother, and father, and been an agonizing witness to my mother's despair. I had walked trembling through jeering crowds shouting *"Juden, Juden,"* seen their loathing, flinched at their howls and screams and threats. I had seen Jews of all ages, from all levels of society, being herded together and moved en masse into crowded living arrangements that felt precarious and temporary. I had witnessed what happened to my father—how someone, or something, had taken him away from us and broken him—and in my own childish way I had tried to deal with the mysterious question of his death. I also witnessed how our Jewish neighbors from our building and our best friends from Wiener Neustadt were taken away and never returned. I had become a keen observer, realizing my survival depended on being constantly on guard.

At an age when most children still trust the adults around them, I had developed an almost sixth sense about the dangers of the society in which we tried so hard to stay invisible. Playing in the streets, riding the streetcar or underground, even walking along beside my mother, in situations where most children feel safe in familiar surroundings, I had already developed an extraordinary awareness of hostile or questioning glances, of the presence or absence of authorities, of all the danger signals that could lead to sudden, violent, and arbitrary disruption of our precarious existence.

My life was focused on my family and our home at Herminengasse 15. The larger world was comprised of those other districts of Vienna where we had to go out of necessity—to visit my mother's relatives and shop for necessities. But there were many times when we took another excursion—to visit the Jewish cemetery where my father was buried.

Mother made each cemetery visit seem like a country outing. We usually brought our lunch and ate on one of the benches. Even in the war days, the Jewish cemetery was a beautiful great park, and in visiting it, I was conscious of the many famous people buried there. We loved to read the inscriptions on the stones. Maxi's favorite was the gravestone of the famous Jewish opera coloratura Elizza Frei. Her gravestone was the sculpture of a tree with a little bird sitting under it. The inscription on the stone read: *"Nur der Schoenheit weiht' ich mein Leben (vizi d'arte)"* ("Only to art I dedicated my life"), taken from the aria of the opera *Tosca*.

Although the part of the cemetery we visited was clearly labeled as Jewish, we did not feel in much danger. A portion of the cemetery grounds had been turned into vegetable gardens used by the military. Jewish people were drafted to work the gardens. (Willie, our neighbor, was one of the workers there during the war.) The cemetery was in the 11th District, a blue-collar area some distance from the center of Vienna where the movements of civilians were not that closely monitored.

Apart from these cemetery visits, the farthest I traveled from home during the war was to visit my mother's family in Burgenland. That would be the extent of my view of the world outside Vienna.

• • • • •

I know that my family, including my brother, must have tried as much as possible to protect me and my sister from the Nazi menace that seemed to be trying to invade every aspect of our lives. We didn't have our own radio to listen to. We could not trust the newspapers, because Hitler's defeats were never reported there. I was only dimly aware—if at all—of the invasion of neighboring countries, of the futile efforts made by other governments to appease the Führer, or the horrific machine that had been set in motion to purge the Aryan world of Jews, gypsies, homosexuals, and other "undesirables."

What did reach my young ears, a mantra that spelled the difference between hope and despair, was the frequently repeated word "visas." Not until after the war, when I found out who survived and who perished, did I fully understand why these documents were so important. For Austrian Jews a visa offered the one possibility of winning safe exit from the country. Despite the rampant anti-Semitism that had convulsed the nation and permeated many layers of government, the bureaucracy remained intact. A visa, accompanied by a great deal of money, was the one way to get through that bureaucracy. Any visa obtained from Western Europe, England, or (most valuable of all) the United States, was potentially a ticket to freedom. What I now realize, though I did not know the details then, are the extraordinary measures that my relatives took to obtain those precious pieces of paper. Every possible connection was used—friends, family members, or professional associates living outside the country—in order to initiate an application. What followed were extortionate payments to government officials (most of one's life savings) and standing in long lines to obtain the right to stand in other long lines. And, always, waiting, waiting.

Uncle Bernhard and Aunt Sarah (who first took us in when we were moved to Vienna), along with their three daughters, were among those who finally succeeded in obtaining visas for the United States. Though during the war, I heard only a smattering of information about where they moved, afterward I was able to reconstruct how they managed to make their escape before all exit routes were finally closed off to Jews.

By the time my own family moved to Vienna, their daughter, Frieda, had emigrated to the United States with her husband and young daughter. (They had been able to get visas through her husband's family.) Once in the States, Frieda immediately went to work getting visas for the rest of the family. Through her efforts Uncle Bernhard, Aunt Sarah, Cousin Else, and Cousin Bertha finally obtained visas. (Even with these visas in hand, my Uncle Bernhard would have had to pay enormous sums in "back taxes" to the authorities—money deliberately extorted by the Nazis from any Jews leaving the country.)

My cousins Else and Bertha, who could exit on a family visa, faced an agonizing choice. Both their husbands had been arrested (at different times) and sent to the concentration camp at Dachau. The only conceivable way to obtain a release for these men was to obtain exit visas for them. That would have been impossible to arrange by anyone living outside the country. But the visas allowing Else and Bertha to exit Austria had a time limit. If they stayed behind and tried to get visas for their husbands in Dachau, they might all be trapped.

Faced with these unimaginable choices, Else and Bertha each made different decisions. Bertha decided to leave with little Eric. If she did not seize her one opportunity to leave the country with Eric, it was unlikely they would have a second chance. In the end, Bertha and Eric joined Uncle Bernhard and Aunt Sarah and emigrated to the United States. Eric was only three years old when he last saw his father. (What we heard later is that his father tried to escape from the camp but was caught and did not survive. No one knows how and where he died.)

For Else the circumstances were somewhat different. She and Martin had no children. Else made the decision to forfeit her visa to the U.S., but she did so with the hope that by remaining in Vienna, she would finally succeed in getting Martin's release from Dachau. She said her farewells to her parents, sister, and nephew, not knowing whether she would ever see them again. Then she redoubled her efforts to obtain a visa that would cover Martin as well as her. And she finally succeeded, but only by the narrowest of margins. Else had a close friend in Sweden, and the friend finally obtained an exit visa for Else that included Martin. Else and Martin first sailed to Sweden and, soon after, emigrated to the U.S., joining the Bauer family in New York.

Of course, all this I had to reconstruct many years later. I only knew that people were leaving—Uncle Bernhard, Aunt Sarah, Cousin Bertha, and darling little Eric. And I would later learn that two more of Uncle Bernhard's children, Julius and Johanna, had the opportunity to leave for Argentina, where they survived the war.

But I don't remember the farewells, if there were any. Once their visas were approved, people had to disappear as quickly and as quietly as possible for fear that officials might change their minds, that their papers might be challenged, or that orders might for some reason be contravened by higher authorities. I'm sure I saw my wonderful cousin Else from time to time after the others left, but once her Swedish visa came through, she, too, was finally gone.

Tante Rosa

Another émigré of that period was Aunt Rosa, who, as I have mentioned, had lived all her life in Stoettera and ran the country store after my grandfather died. At first, my aunt thought she would be better off if she moved to Vienna, where she might be less conspicuous, rather than staying on as the only Jew in a small village. She closed the store, locked up the house, and left with all her cash, which, I understand, was quite a small fortune in those days. As Aunt Rosa was approaching the bus stop for Vienna, the Austrian *Gendarmie* were already waiting for her, apparently tipped off by one of her neighbors. She was arrested and her money was confiscated. Somehow, though, she was able to get released, and eventually managed to immigrate to Portugal, where she was interned during the war, along with a number of other Austrian Jews.

• • • • •

From the way conversations dwelled on the subject, I knew that a visa spelled hope. But I also understood that there was little or no chance that my own immediate family—a mother with her three young children—could ever obtain one of those precious documents. Those who had escaped were now living the life of struggling immigrants in faraway countries. There was no way they could guarantee support for us, and that was a prerequisite of getting any kind of visa.

As Nazi rule tightened, countries like England and the United States decided to offer no special dispensation to fleeing Jews. To the foreign officials who made these life-and-death decisions, an impoverished mother with three children were the least likely candidates for a visa. We knew we had no recourse but to remain where we were.

The word never quite vanished from adult conversation. But for all it meant to us as a family, getting a visa was nothing more than a fantasy.

· · · · ·

Before the war, there were about 113,000 Jews in Vienna.* Through 1939, Adolf Eichmann, who headed the office for central immigration in Vienna, undertook a ruthless program to extort cash and possessions from any Jews ultimately permitted to emigrate. By the end of October 1939, there were 66,000 residents defined as Jews or "race-Jews" remaining in Vienna. In 1940, Hitler decreed that

---

* This statistic comes from United States Memorial Holocaust Encyclopedia entry for "Vienna."

all the remaining Jews in Austria should be deported to Poland. These deportations, first to Poland and then directly to the death camps, began in 1941 and continued throughout the war.

From Max's notes: "All our friends are now driven away to the East; we become isolated in an 'Aryan' neighborhood. In the beginning, we even received some cards from them. Later, no more signs of life from them. . . . We think that due to the war, no postal service is working. How wrong we were. . . ."

· · · · ·

World War II is said to have begun on September 1, 1939, when Hitler's army invaded Poland. But by then, we were already living with the reality of Nazi rule. The onset of the war meant to us that our last connections with the outside world were severed.

By the end of 1939 there was not even a remote possibility that we would find means of escape. Our only hope was to exercise caution, remain vigilant, and—as the years passed—look forward to the one possibility of release: the end of the war.

CHAPTER 12

Vienna's Second District

FOR MY MOTHER THERE WAS A TERRIBLE IRONY IN our situation. Under any other circumstances she would have loved Vienna. Though born and raised on a farm, she was never a "country girl." Given her love of glamour, music, dancing, and gracious living, I'm sure she would eventually have moved to the city where she was now forced to live. Vienna was beautiful before the war (and is again, today, after decades of restoration and rebuilding). It was the capital for European academics, artists, writers, musicians, and intellectuals. And a great number of these educated people were Jewish, with big names in medicine, literature, music, etcetera.

The Second District, where we had to live in anonymity, was probably the least desirable area of the city. Buildings like ours in this district were functional workshops or tenements, architecturally undistinguished, and the population was mostly working class. At the beginning of the war, it was the only district where Jews were allowed to live. But the districts of Vienna where my mother would have wanted to live, had she a choice, were far more splendid.

In our neighborhood it was customary for residents and shop keepers to take up their daily posts on their door stoops or on the street to share neighborhood gossip, rumors, or grievances. My mother was averse to these exchanges and shied mostly away from contact. I recall how our next-door neighbor, Frau Churan, kept trying to engage her in conversation, mostly in vain. I was an easier target, however.

In fact, I loved spending time with Frau Churan. She was certainly no beauty: to me the short woman seemed extremely homely. But perhaps it was because of that—in some way to compensate for her plainness—she was utterly full of charm. (Her very handsome husband, everyone assumed, had somehow overlooked her homeliness and been won by her remarkable charisma.) I liked talking to Frau Churan and also enjoyed playing with her two young children, Helli and Karli.

I distinctly recall the day Frau Churan won my unending devotion and loyalty. I am sure she had noted—who could help it?—the radiant beauty of my sister, Lilly. In the middle of her teen years, Lilly had a full figure, lovely complexion, reddish hair, and the kind of prettiness that made young men turn around instantly and pay attention to her. I, by contrast, had a skinny, tomboyish figure, incomparably different, and (in my own eyes) was inferior to my older sister. Not only that, I knew Frau Churan had caught a glimpse of me at my very worst—the day when my mother had rubbed petroleum jelly into my hair and wrapped my head in a bulky towel in an attempt to drive out an infestation of lice.

Imagine my astonishment and delight when, just then, Frau Churan took me aside to reassure me: "Katharina, some day you will be much more beautiful than your sister!"

Whether or not I completely believed her, those words have remained with me ever since.

• • • • •

Though, as I mentioned, my mother was not one to stand on the street and gossip, she did have one very close friend, Frau Prantl, who moved into Herminengasse 13, the house next door to ours. Frau Prantl came from Stoettera, the town where my father had grown up, and my mother, knowing her from earlier days, must have felt that she could confide in her. To me Frau Prantl seemed like a charming, chubby country lady who also preferred to live in the city. I knew she was a widow—her husband had been killed in the First World War—and she had several daughters. To hide her age, she always dyed her hair jet black. It was no secret that Frau Prantl always had a boyfriend, and it was in her nature to talk quite openly about him even in my presence. I recall her saying, in reference to her gentleman friend, that she liked this one quite a bit, but he had no intention of having a serious relationship with her since she had too many dependents—meaning daughters and grandchildren.

Mama usually went to Frau Prantl's house to chat, and I missed overhearing most of their conversations. Not until many decades later did I learn about one of the confidences that my mother shared. She apparently told Frau Prantl that she had met a well-educated man named Herr Schloegl in the bakery, which was apparently followed by other meetings. The upshot was, my mother arranged for me to have some private lessons with Herr Schloegl in math and other subjects.

I remember visiting a dingy apartment just a few blocks away from our building, where I was greeted by a man whose looks, today, I would compare to those of Woody Allen (although Herr Schloegl was somewhat taller, a little heavier—but he did have those very thick glasses). I knew he was a widower, and he had a son about my age who went to regular school.

I forget the content of those lessons, and I don't think I visited Herr Schloegl very often, but I was abruptly reminded of him just a couple of years ago. Shortly before Maxi's death, he and I were talking about my mother, and I wondered aloud why she never remarried or had any relationship (that I knew of) after our father died.

"But she did!" said Max. "She had a boyfriend in Vienna during the war."

I was in shock. How could Lilly and I have been so innocent, not to have known something like that?

"Who was it?"

"You remember Herr Schloegl, don't you?"

From some remark dropped by Frau Prantl, Max had learned that my tutor had been Mama's "boyfriend." Given Frau Prantl's willingness to talk about her own affairs, I'm sure she was the one person my mother felt easy confiding in. But sometime during the war, something happened. Their friendship ended abruptly, and Mama's visits to Herminengasse 13 came to an end. Could it have been because of Frau Prantl's indiscretion in mentioning Herr Schloegl to my brother? Quite possibly, but of course I'll never know for sure.

• • • • •

Though we were a tightly knit family, Max, Lilly, and I had very different personalities. Before we moved to Vienna (when Max had to give up his studies), he was a serious student. In Wiener Neustadt, he had excelled in all subjects, including religion. But, as he explains it, "When the school year ends in 1938, I am 'invited' to leave school prematurely, for good. In other words, I am thrown out (and I am only fourteen years old). The report card, *Zeugnis*, show that I was an A student."

Since I could not go to school, he tried to give me home lessons in subjects like reading and writing. Like Max, I loved to learn new things, so I think he liked tutoring me from time to time.

Lilly, though never studious, had a wonderful talent for knitting and sewing, which she loved to do. With meticulous needlework, she created little dress-up items for the tiny, finger-length dolls we played with in those days. When it was impossible to find full skeins of yarn, Lilly would gather together fragments of knitted clothes, unravel the yarn, then use the longest pieces to knit scarves, hats, and sweaters in a multitude of colors.

Yet my sister was no shrinking violet. I vividly recall a time she and I went sledding together nearby on a downhill road that was not much used, and a number of boys began bothering us. I don't know whether they were just trying to get Lilly's attention—a frequent occurrence—or whether they just made a practice of teasing any girls who came along. In any case, they went too far. Before I quite knew what was happening, I was treated to the sight of my older sister viciously swinging her sled back and forth as she advanced on the obstreperous gang, protecting us both. They backed off. I was impressed! I learned to use similar methods myself on other occasions when I was on my own.

(There was also a memorable and frightening incident after the war, when we both took the train to the country to fetch some food. Lovely Lilly was approached by several young men on the train. Apparently thinking they would impress her, they began bragging about serving as soldiers in Hitler's army, showing us pictures of them and their friends in their uniforms. When they expressed regret that some of those friends had died in action, my sister turned on them and said, "Good, they should have died." I was horrified and feared instant retribution, but like the roughnecks who had faced my sled-wielding sister, the former solders kept their distance.)

I was a curious and very energetic child. I couldn't sit still, and it seemed like I was often the one my mother had to discipline. I always got along with Max. I looked up to him and I saw him as my protector. Not so with Lilly. We often fought—mostly about childish stuff, like who should sit on what chair or who could play with a certain toy. She also had her fights with Maxi, and she would easily get physical, starting to kick him for one reason or another. As fragile as she was always made out to be, she was actually quite tough, and proved so in later years. (However, as we all grew older, Lilly became very close to Max. Whenever they would meet, either in New York or Vienna, however, and Max would bring up the subject of the war years, Lilly would interrupt him: "Maxi, if you try to walk down Memory Lane again, I am leaving!" She would react the same way toward me whenever I brought up those times, even when I would touch on the more pleasant memories, such as our liberation. Lilly was the first person I offered a draft of this manuscript to read. I felt that with the perspective of having been two years older than I, she might be able to point out some gaps in the story or offer a different viewpoint. Her immediate reaction was "I don't have to read it—I've been there.")

Lilly in Vienna, 1943.

I'm sure I was irritated by the favoritism shown to Lilly as well as by her wonderful looks. Only in later years, when we were both teenagers, did we reach a kind of truce, and then it was because she had secrets she wanted to share (mostly about boys), and I became her confidante. Then I was her ally and best friend, and by that time we had totally given up the kind of fights that children often get into. We became close, and more serious. I believe that our survival of the war made us a very close family.

• • • • •

While Max had the joys of the opera to feed his cultural tastes, as already mentioned, we were without a gramophone or radio. Even without recorded music, though, my mother was determined that she would teach us how to waltz. She simply sang or hummed the music to accompany our steps. This was the perfect way to imagine herself in a place where she really wanted to be, the far-distant (to us) Viennese ballrooms where regally dressed people waltzed to the strains of string quartets.

The waltz was the only dance my mother knew, but she was superb at it. I too was a quick learner, and my mother was very impressed by how deftly I could adapt my steps when we switched position and I could do the left-turn waltz just as gracefully as the right-turn waltz. It was, in many ways, her old-fashioned way of preparing her girls for a future social life. (Later on, I developed the desire to become a dancer, which was quickly discouraged by my mother: "Dancing is fine for short-term enjoyment, but not as a lifetime profession.")

As for Max, he was quite clumsy when it came to dance. At first mother tried to get him to join in our waltz sessions, but ultimately she had to acknowledge that it was useless. I'm sure he was relieved when she gave up. He could return to his books and leave us to our waltz lesson. (Little did he realize she was not quite done with him. After the war, Mama would make one final attempt by sending Maxi to a ballroom dance school. My brother admitted that it "helped a little." Later in life, when his grand-nieces dragged him out onto the dance floor, he would happily comply, commenting with a gleam in his eyes, "They seduced me!")

• • • • •

My brother also taught me chess. He was a formidable challenger, and we often played together in the evenings. (He continued to play the game throughout his life.)

There was another game that we played frequently, a very popular German board game called *"Mensch äergere dich nicht"* (which translates literally as "Do Not Get Angry, Man") that could be played with three or four people. The board is in the shape of a plus sign, and each player gets six colored pieces that, at the start, are lined up in a row toward the center. Marching around the board with each throw of a dice, pieces are moved in a clockwise direction. The objective is to get all the way around the board and return all pieces to the "home base" before anyone else. The title of the game came into play when, by the rule of the game, you arrived at a certain spot close to the finish and there was a penalty causing you to start all over again from the base.

Lilly and I were combative enough that we each allowed ourselves to gloat when we won.

• • • • •

Our home had the advantage of great privacy, and within its boundaries we felt safe observing all the Jewish holidays. My brother knew his Hebrew, and my mother followed the traditions of Hannukah, Passover, and most of the Jewish holidays with all the fidelity of a convert who had studied carefully and learned her lessons well. Hannukah came and went without the gifts, and when we celebrated Seder, most of the traditional foods were missing. But otherwise we did everything possible to recognize the important rituals of our faith.

CHAPTER 13

Necessary Country Visits

I DOUBT THAT MY MOTHER'S FAMILY EVER GOT completely used to the idea of her marrying a Jewish man, but after my father's death there was an important reconciliation with her Catholic family. This was fortunate for all of us, but particularly for me. It meant that Mama began making monthly visits to her family's farm in Zagersdorf. "Food is scarce," writes Max, "but our country relatives help us a lot and we don't starve. In the middle of the year for the first time, we hear from a distant relative of our mother, whose main job is to 'contraband' food to her friends and customers, that the Jews who were deported to the east are being 'gassed' in special concentration camps. We do not believe this at first, but on the other side, we don't get a sign of life from all our friends who were deported."

I always accompanied Mama on her trips, and looking back, I think there were a number of reasons why I outranked Lilly or Max for these expeditions. I'm sure Mama felt it was good to have a skinny, waiflike little child along to instill sympathy in anyone who might be paying attention. If Max had come along, he would have been noticed as a healthy young man looking eligible for the army. And Lilly was probably considered too delicate to make the arduous walks that were part of the journey.

Another factor, I am sure, is that Mama knew I was apt to get into trouble if I stayed at home. Max and Lilly might have their disagreements, but at least they could be relied on to obey instructions. Mama knew I would be quite likely to venture out to the street by myself and probably get into trouble if I was left behind.

There was a routine aspect to these monthly journeys. We rarely took the bus. Usually, it was a slow train ride lasting about two hours, with stops at all the rural stations. Mama and I debarked either at Drasburg (if we were going straight to the farm) or Wulkerprodersdorf (if we were first visiting the aunt and uncle in Antau). From either town we faced another forty-five-minute walk from and to the train, bearing our rucksacks both ways.

On our way back to the station, many times we stopped and picked wild roschip berries from the bushes. From these free pickings, Mama would make delicious jam. Of course, this added to the weight of the rucksacks, and even though I was impatient about having another chore (picking rosehip berries from the thorny bushes) I enjoyed what I knew would be the outcome—delicious rosehip jam.

The family farm where we stayed had no electricity, running water, or plumbing. My aunt, a thin woman with a sweet voice, cooked on a wood stove in the large kitchen where the whole family gathered for the largest daily meal. Water came from a well; we used an outhouse when we had to go to the toilet. In the evening the house was lit with oil lamps.

In the back of the house was a huge grove of fruit trees that bore abundantly in season—cherries, plums, apricots, and apples. There was a productive vineyard, and if we visited at the right time of year, my mother and I would help pick the grapes for winemaking in exchange for grapes to take home. I may have helped out, but there were also rewards. I would sometimes sit in the middle of the vineyard and gorge myself on the ripe grapes, occasionally plucking peaches from the peach trees that were interplanted among the vines. I saw little of my sturdy uncle, since he was usually out toiling in the fields, but I became very close to my cousins Schanko and his little sister, Maritza. Thus began a relationship that would form into a lasting bond for the rest of our lives.

I was perfectly happy with these ventures into the country since they meant I would get to meet up with aunts and uncles and cousins that I rarely saw, lend a hand at the farm, and sleep in the embrace of a puffy featherbed in a room shared with my cousins. Mama and I always carried rucksacks on these journeys—hers much bigger than mine, of course—and they were filled to capacity both coming and going. Outbound from Vienna, Mama stuffed the packs with items that were available in Vienna but not in the country—used clothing or materials needed on the farm. Especially valued was a pesticide called *Kupfervitriol*, which my brother Max brought from his munitions factory job. (Of course this had to be done in secret, since that material was used for the manufacture of munitions.) In exchange, he would bring back food to the beautiful Frau Deutsch. She obviously knew that what she was doing was illegal. This *Kupfervitriol* was to be used to produce munitions against Germany's enemies. I do not know how

Frau Deutsch and Max communicated about this, as I was very young. Maxi may have explained it to mother but not to us children. Only after the war did I learn why Frau Deutsch was the way she was—quite unique.

On the return trip from the country, our rucksacks were filled to capacity with all the food we could possibly carry, including potatoes, fruit, and at least one bottle of wine from the vineyard. The last was expressly intended as a "gift" to our superintendent, Herr Vicecka, to keep him quiet and encourage him to remain always on our side.

I was a willing porter but must have been a somewhat pitiful sight to others. During one of our long walks to the station along the hot and dusty road, one passerby looked in horror at the little, sweaty, red-faced girl—my neck was bulging with the strain of the load—and chastised my mother for "using a child" to carry such a heavy burden. But I understood the necessity of these missions to the country. Some of the gleanings were for our own use, of course, but more than half were reserved for special gifts—mostly bribes to assure that others would not reveal our identity. Always, a portion of the fresh produce went to our protector, who had essentially become our savior by intervening in the matter of the food ration cards and the advice of not wearing the yellow star. As the war continued and shortages grew worse, our farm-fresh commodities were highly prized.

My mother was far less enchanted with country life than I. In fact, in later years she frequently repeated how she hated the country—and she told us we must make absolutely sure she was not to be buried in the cemetery that practically bordered the family's property. But I think she was relieved to be reunited with her family, and though she was not always able to get everything they wanted, she was generous in her efforts to try to bring what they most needed from the city. Since the farm held no charms for Mama, almost from the moment of our arrival she would begin seeking out neighbors and relatives in the village. She had lengthy chats with them, often in Croatian, about Vienna, the war, or family matters. I was dragged along to keep me out of trouble, so there was nothing I could do but wait restlessly until the adults had finished their conversations, so boring in my little mind. I was surprised they never asked questions about my father or about our faith; or, perhaps they did ask, and mother answered in Croatian (which I did not understand).

There was sure compensation, however, for enduring these long talks. Before long I would begin tugging at my mother's hand, asking for "the apples." In time the reward came. When Mama could shush me no more, I would be temporarily silenced by being given one of the delicious, semi-dried, out-of-season apples that villagers stored in the attic under dry straw to keep them from freezing in the winter. This would keep me quiet for a while. I was always hungry, even in the country.

• • • • •

On one occasion I thought I was lucky enough to visit the country entirely by myself. Though the visit did not end as I would have wished, it was memorable. Living in Antau were Aunt Anna and her estranged husband (who was also, unfortunately, a hopeless alcoholic and the bane of my aunt's existence). They had three daughters, one of whom was Hilda, the cousin who lived in Vienna. It was Hilda's baby son, Peter, for whom I babysat during my "school" mornings, and when Hilda and her family were going to visit Aunt Anna, I was invited along as a companion for little Peter.

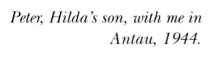

Peter, Hilda's son, with me in Antau, 1944.

Aunt Anna, to my delight, was wonderfully tuned in to children. She had often visited us in Vienna, brought us food, and we all adored her. I recall the first night in Antau when she thought I might enjoy the treat of sleeping all by myself in their small house adjoining the main house. She showed me the private room where I was to sleep, probably expecting me to be thrilled, but something in my expression must have signaled alarm. A strange, lonely house in a far-away village—it was all too scary! How she sensed my fear I don't know, but she immediately responded to my hesitation and, instead, offered to let me share her big bed in the main house. I readily accepted. I was so happy—and slept soundly.

CHAPTER 14

Shepherd Girl and Pony Tender

A BIG JOY IN ANTAU WAS MY NEW EXPERIENCE AS A "shepherd girl." My aunt and uncle had a number of cows that they kept in a nearby meadow. Those cows were docile beasts, but grazing in an open area without walls or fencing, they had a tendency to wander off. Someone had to stand by and wield a small whip to persuade them to stay in their pasture. This duty I eagerly accepted but soon discovered that tending cows was not as easy as it looked. The cows knew very well that I was new to this and persistently made forays from their assigned pasture into the neighbor's property where, most likely, there was more and better grass to munch on. I had to be after them constantly. I didn't mind that. It kept me extremely busy. But by the end of the day I was totally exhausted. This was far from cow-tending as I imagined it and had seen it portrayed in paintings—the pastoral scenes in which a young shepherd sits idly by, playing his flute, with scarcely a glance at the contented cows under his supervision. I could not sit down for a moment when those beasts took advantage of a newcomer like me and kept wandering off. I had to admit I was relieved when finally the adults took over my new "job." But my venture into cow-herding, like so many of my "enterprises," was emblematic of a streak in my nature. I wanted to do *everything* and do it as well as I could. For a few days, all my ambitions had been focused on being a good shepherd girl.

I could easily have stayed the full week in Antau, sleeping in the big featherbed with my wonderful aunt, cheerfully looking after little Peter, and occasionally playing shepherdess to the restless cows who I hoped would better themselves. But several days into the visit, an incident in the village gave me a shock.

Antau was a pleasant village with sidewalks bordering the main street. In previous visits I had felt perfectly safe exploring on my own. This day was no different, until, suddenly, as I was passing by a farmhouse, I heard the scream *"Juden! Juden!"* coming out from somewhere in back. I whirled around. Whoever had shouted at me had vanished. Turning on my heel, I ran as fast as I could back to the safety of Aunt Anna's house. Once there, I said nothing to anyone. But I was terrified.

Somehow the news of the incident reached my mother. She came and got me at once and brought me back home to Vienna.

• • • • •

For a child like me—hungry for adventure, always eager to explore—Vienna's huge outdoor park, the Prater, was a gift at my doorstep. The Prater bordered the Second District with acres of green lawns, walking paths, and best of all, a full-scale amusement park with an enormous Ferris wheel (the *Riesenrad*), a waterslide, funhouse, elaborately designed arcades, and a pony carousel. When I first visited with Lilly, she expressed to me she would rather walk the *Rotenturmstrasse,* the "fashion street," where her attention was transfixed by the window displays.

Walking and looking were not enough for me, and I was too young to be entranced with fashion. I had to be more occupied by doing things. It was not until I ventured by myself into the Prater that I began to get a real sample of its wonders. Next to the pony carousel was an area with children's swings shaped like small boats. To my amazement I saw someone I knew there—Inge, a friend who had attended some classes with me in the makeshift school, a former synagogue, that we went to for a short while until it also had to close. She was helping out by pushing the children on the boat swings, giving their mothers some time off to stand by and gossip among themselves. As Inge braked the boats and helped the children out, I noticed the mothers who paid the fare for their children would also reward Inge with a few extra pennies. I immediately got interested.

"Do you think I can do this with you?" I asked.

Inge agreed right away. She liked having company. "Of course!" she replied. "And I'm not here all the time. Then you can do it by yourself."

She introduced me to the owners—the Reinprecht family.

With that, I became Inge's assistant. We shared the five-penny tips, and she told me which afternoons she had to miss so I could take over for her. The children were cute, playful, and happy. The mothers preferred to chat with one another and left the swinging of the children to us. And I was proud to earn a little money, especially on the days when Inge could not come.

Better things were to come! Not far from the boat swings was the pony carousel, also a Reinprecht family property and a premier attraction for children. It was expensive compared to the boat swings—approximately one mark per ride. But this was no ordinary carousel. The elaborately gilded coaches that went round and round to the sound of organ music were pulled by *live ponies*. Older children assisted in helping the young ones in and out of the coaches. Others held them on the saddles of the riding ponies (since a few of them walked next to the coaches and horses). I was enthralled. Already an experienced boat-swing pusher, I instantly saw my future as a carousel assistant. I volunteered to help.

Contemporary photograph showing the Wiener Ponny-Caroussel in the Prater, which has remained remarkably well preserved. This is almost exactly how it appeared in the early 1940s when I was there.

As it turned out, my services were needed. I was quick and agile. I could dart between the carriages and horses even when they were moving. All my babysitting experience came into play as I helped the little children. Most glorious of all, I got as many free rides as I wanted.

Since the ride was expensive, tips were more generous. By the end of an afternoon, I had nearly two marks clutched in my hand—enough, in those days, to buy milk and bread. Suddenly my income had leapt from the realm of pennies to the stratosphere of marks. Gleefully, I showed the earnings to my mother.

To my chagrin Mama was horrified rather than pleased. Her daughter was now visible to the thousands of Viennese who thronged to the Prater. It was only a matter of time before I would be stopped and questioned, the discovery made that I was Jewish and not wearing the yellow star, and *then what?* We could all be deported! My mother told me I was absolutely, never again, to visit the Prater by myself.

In typical fashion, I disobeyed. The pony carousel was far too exciting and too important to sacrifice. And I felt comfortable with my "employers." The ponies and the carousel as well as the swings had been owned for generations by the Reinprecht family, which had obviously prospered from this enterprise. They had three daughters—Erna, the eldest; then Irma; and Maria, the youngest (she was my age). All went to higher schools *(Gymnasium)*. Many afternoons one or the other would deck themselves out in dresses with fur trimmings and go to the opera or to a theater.

Frau Reinprecht was a likable, matronly woman, probably in her early fifties, who spoke German in the Viennese dialect (though she was a woman of few words). Her husband, younger looking than her, was very handsome and elegant. In the beginning, they expected me to turn over the fares I had collected after each ride, which entailed a lot of running back and forth after each round of collections. But as they came to trust me, this was no longer necessary. I could accumulate the fares, then hand them over to Frau Reinprecht after a number of rides. She would open the window of their house and I handed her the money collection.

I knew I was good at this! It was thrilling to dodge among the carriages and live ponies. The mothers saw how carefully I helped their children—and showed their appreciation. And at the same time, I was invisible, just another one of numerous children in the Prater Park. Where was the risk?

My mother and I fought a battle of wills. She forbade me to go: "They will discover you are Jewish. We will all be arrested and wind up in Auschwitz!"

"No one knows!" I protested. "Nothing will happen!"

I returned home safely each day, exhilarated by the sights and sounds of the Prater, with my earnings in hand. Gradually, my mother gave in. After a week or so there was a turnaround. Not only would I be allowed to continue—Mama now started to like the extra monies she received almost daily. A few extra marks were a welcome addition to the family income, which consisted of Max's meager salary and whatever small side jobs Mama could obtain, helping families with housework.

With typical contrariness, that was just about the time I began to lose interest. Some of the glamour had worn off, and *being expected* to "work" every afternoon was not the same as enjoying a surreptitious adventure. Now I had become, literally, one of the "breadwinners" in the family. Nevertheless, I went along with my mother's change of heart and continued to show up faithfully at the carousel. Even though the sense of excitement was never quite the same, the truth is I felt very grown up, accomplished, and important. Just as I had striven to be a good shepherdess, I was now embarked on becoming an earner in my new vocation.

Unfortunately it was not to last—and, again, it was the threat of discovery that brought my carousel career to an end. The people I saw most often at the Prater were the Reinprechts, and as with anyone I encountered frequently, I had to make an assessment of what they knew and what they believed about me. I was careful never to appear at the carousel during school hours. When I was with the daughters, I always pretended that I had been busy all morning with school classes, just like them. But if my secret was to remain undiscovered, I would have to create a consistent story about classes, schoolmates, and teachers. This became much more difficult when Maria, who was my age, began to ask what I was learning in my school.

I worried about this. Then I told my mother. What she had feared had now come to pass. We didn't know whether the Reinprechts already knew, or suspected, that I came from a Jewish family—but that was just the problem. What if they found out and they were actually Nazi sympathizers? What if Maria began to guess that I really did not go to school? What if she told her parents and they began to ask questions?

Mama, Max, and I concluded that I would be tempting fate if I continued to show up at the carousel. I simply stopped going, and the Reinprechts did not know where to contact me and possibly never tried. They had never asked for an address or telephone number (which I could not have given them anyway, since we had no phone). We would miss the income. And I would miss my adventures at the Prater (even though it had already lost some of its attraction for me). I was sorry that, once again, I had to disappear from sight. But I understood why it was necessary.

CHAPTER 15

In the Ruins of Vienna

DURING THE WINTERS OF THOSE WAR YEARS, I WAS often cold and hungry. Since I was skinny and very active, I'm sure the chill and the hunger were related to high metabolism and low body fat. But it was also the case that the Austrian winters were bitterly cold, with biting wind and almost constant snow, and our apartment had meager heat. I still have a mental picture of Mama, Max, Lilly, and I around the little coal-burning stove in the one room that served as our bedroom/living room. We are all wearing our winter clothing and our hands are outstretched, palms down, as we try to absorb the scant warmth from the stove and keep the cold at our backs.

Even our petroleum lamp could provide some heat if you held your hands close to it. But I discovered it was impractical to count on the lamp as a real heat source. Its fuel was the cheapest petroleum, and whenever the lamp was turned up high, it would start smoking; the white glass cylinder immediately darkened with soot. So Mama insisted we keep the lamp turned down to a small flame, using it for light rather than heat.

Though our living quarters were small, there were numerous chores to be done. Our days began early. Stoves had to be lit, and that meant bringing in wood or coal from the cellar. Water had to be heated for the breakfast. Milk and bread were bought fresh every morning, which meant brisk walks to the milk store and the bakery, two different stores. Immediately following breakfast, there were dishes to wash, and then another round of hot water to heat up so we could wash ourselves.

Everything for the main meal, lunch, had to be prepared by hand. It was impossible to get a week's worth of vegetables at the market (and in any case, that wasn't the custom in those days), so Mama had to make separate trips, each day, to find whatever was available. After shopping, the food had to be cleaned, cut, chopped, and prepared. And with four people living in such a small space, the apartment had to be cleaned daily. Each day, it seemed, there were scarcely enough hours to accomplish all that had to be done with housework alone.

· · · · ·

Meals were meager, but always on time. On Sundays, when Max was not working, we knew Mama would serve lunch exactly at noon and that we were expected to be at the table, ready to eat. She would not tolerate anyone being late. Mama felt she worked hard to get a meal together, and she did not want it to get cold. This was especially true of those occasions when she had cooked some of the precious meat brought in from the country.

Our morning breakfast, served by Mama at 7:00 a.m. sharp, was always the same fare, somewhat less than what we would today consider a continental breakfast. For the adults, Mama and Max, there was coffee and a piece of bread with some butter if we had it. Lilly and I quite often had hot chocolate.

Providing us with hot chocolate required some inventiveness on my mother's part. Though I cannot quite remember all the details, I know Mama must have used some substitute like powdered cacao in its preparation, since chocolate or chocolate candy were unavailable throughout the war. (I'm sure there was real chocolate in Vienna—what would that city be without it?—but it was unobtainable for us. Only German soldiers were able to get it for their families.) After Mama got us all up for breakfast, she would quickly make all the beds to eliminate the risk of anyone going back to bed.

The most difficult challenge of preparing hot chocolate was the heating and straining of milk. At the time there was no homogenized or pasteurized milk, so the milk had to be boiled. You knew it was boiling when a skin formed and the milk started to rise, but then you had to quickly get it off the stove before it boiled over. We children hated it when a film of skin was swimming around in the hot chocolate, and Mama accommodated us by putting the milk through a strainer before mixing it with the cocoa.

The milk-boiling part of this process required special attention. Mama was not always successful in rescuing the pan from the stove before it boiled over. When it did overflow, there was a mess, and Mama would mumble a number of choice words that were neither German nor Croatian, but Hungarian. *"Bassa matja!"* was one of the phrases I recall.

(Mama never cursed, and I was in for a surprise when I finally discovered the meaning of *"bassa matja!"* Many years later a Hungarian friend told me the mumbled words meant "mother-fucker!" To this day I am convinced Mama really had no idea what she was saying: it was just a foreign-language epithet that helped her blow off steam. At least, that's what I hope!)

• • • • •

Recalling Mama's ingenuity in the creation of our daily meals, I am filled with admiration. Starting with the most basic provisions, she managed to create a main meal at noontime that was truly appetizing. Though we rarely had much meat, Mama could make a tasty goulash by using all the right ingredients, then substituting potatoes for the meat.

Her other specialty for the main meal was a noodle dish pre-pared with flour, potatoes, egg, and water. Mixing these ingre-dients, she kneaded the dough into finger-length rolls that she placed in boiling water. When the pasta was done, she drained off the water and served it with ground poppy seed and sugar. This, along with a bowl of soup, comprised our lunch, which was the main meal each day.

Either at lunch or at evening dinner, we sometimes got *Schmalzbrot,* a piece of dark bread spread with pig lard and lightly sprinkled with some paprika for flavor. The pig's fat in this dish was no ordinary lard: it came from the rendering of freshly slaughtered pigs and was considered "the workers' delicacy." (Though we didn't think of it then, I am sure the high-fat content was valuable in balancing our high-starch, almost meatless, diet.) A *Schmalzbrot* was filling as well as tasty. But when there was no pig's fat available for the making of this dish, Mama served us boiled, salted potatoes for dinner.

There were not many treats, but some Saturdays Mama went early in the morning to the bakery store and brought back plump, warm, fresh-baked rolls and sometimes some *Stollen* (a kind of sweet roll). If we had butter, we would daub a bit of it on the rolls.

When Mama had the ingredients for a sweet dessert, that might become a main meal. I was ecstatic whenever she managed the ultimate—a *Kaiserschmarn*. The name of this crumbly, sweet, delicious Austrian specialty translates literally as "the emperor's mess" or "the emperor's nothing," and tradition holds that it was a favorite of Emperor Franz Joseph I. It is merely a collapsed souf-flé that was supposedly, at one time, a failed dish prepared by the Emperor's chef. According to legend, when the soufflé failed to rise, the chef simply crumbled it and served it as such with pow-dered sugar and raspberry syrup. Ever since, it has been served in Vienna's restaurants as a specialty. The recipe calls for flour, egg yolk, egg whites (stiffly beaten), milk, and salt.

· · · · ·

By seven o'clock on cold winter nights, there was no more reason to stay up. True to mother's farm-based traditions, she damped the stove to preserve the remaining coals. But before doing so, she heated up a rubber hot-water bottle to warm our beds before we crawled in. Each bed got the bottle for a little while.

By eight o'clock I was nestled deep inside my featherbed, the covers piled high around my shoulders. There, at last, I could stop shivering. Only my cheeks and nose were exposed to the frost: the rest of me was enveloped in the cocoon of eider-filled cotton that provided perfect insulation. Before falling asleep, I prayed every night that the war would be over. I always finished with the words *"Lieber Gott beschuetze uns und alle Juden"* ("Dear God, protect us and all Jews").

· · · · ·

Adults frequently talked about the war, and as far as I can recall, there was no time when someone bothered to say "Not in front of the children," or words to that effect. Psychology was not much practiced in those times. (I'm sure the term "child psychology" was foreign to Mama's generation.) One of our "informants" was my warmhearted Aunt Anna. Wartime conditions did not prevent her from making occasional visits to Vienna. Not only was she honest about her need to get away from her alcoholic husband, she was also enthusiastic in her descriptions of whatever handsome man she happened to be seeing during her visits. Oblivious to the impressionable nature of young children, she was as forthcoming about the horrors of war as the pleasures of her personal life. She had charm as well as warmth and charisma, and she loved to talk. It was from her that we first heard that Jews were being sent to the gas chambers. Max remembers: "Jews, being deported

to the East, are being 'gassed' in special concentration camps—
we don't believe these 'atrocity tales' . . . [although] on the other
side, we don't get a sign of life from all those people who were
deported. . . ."

Another information source was the Churan family. Not only
did they have a contraband radio, they also had Frau Churan
to relay frequent updates that came from her husband's gentile
family. Through him Frau Churan had access to information
about the progress of the war. She would talk quietly in a low
voice with my mother—conversations that I could overhear when
I wanted to.

Maxi, too, was politically well informed. Characteristically, he
soaked up every piece of information that came his way. On the
occasions when he could glean any news, he expressed a keen interest in the ebb and flow of the various battles, and one can sense in
his notes the emotions when some small progress was achieved in
the Allies' favor, and his disappointment when campaigns failed or
when things did not happen as fast as we may have wanted.

Max's boss, Frau Deutsch, showed definite signs of having anti-
Hitler leanings, and Max not only listened closely to her, but also
carefully shared his own political views.

Another source for Maxi was the Segen family. When he went
to play chess with Robert, he often returned with news that came
from Robert's father, who had connections and information
which he shared with Max. He did, though, sometimes have to
separate fact from fiction. He would meet almost daily at a neighbor's for informal "rumor gatherings," where young and old men
would discuss the present and the future and the "make-believe":

rumors of premature Allied victories, of Hitler's death, of the war's end. . . .

• • • • •

I realized it was never safe for me to strike up conversations with strangers—it was in my nature to do so—but as long as I acted like a "normal" child and kept to myself pretending to be going on some errand or another, I was sure I would not be bothered. There was actually great irony in the fact that I enjoyed such freedom in my errands around Vienna. In a nation at war, where acts of historical brutality were being perpetrated every hour of the day, a young girl could feel absolutely free to visit any district of Vienna without fear of being harassed, robbed, or molested. In many ways I was terribly innocent, and remained so, even to the end of the war. I had only the vaguest idea of where babies came from, and the concept of rape was foreign to me. (At that age I didn't even know what the word meant.) And it did not seem that Max or Mama were worried about this fact. They were only always worried about being discovered that we were Jewish. I listened, I watched, and I even understood a great deal about what was going on. But in some respects, I was no better informed about the facts of life than any other reader of innocuous children's folk tales. Whether I was alone, trudging through snow at 5:00 a.m. to get Maxi's opera tickets, visiting the carousel at the Prater, or riding the streetcar to visit Cousin Hilda and Peter, I never felt I had to watch out for street criminals. The only real danger—ever present—was that the secret of my Jewish identity would be revealed.

It is another irony that I was not by myself but with my mother when the worst nearly did happen. Loving the world of glamour as she did, my mother had a fascination with certain movie stars. Among her favorites was the young Canadian-born actress Alexis Smith who, in the 1940s, was featured in several Warner Brothers movies opposite Errol Flynn and Fredric March. I don't know the title of the film that found its way past German censors into a Vienna cinema, or why my mother took me along, but for whatever reason I got to see just a bit of Alexis Smith in her full glory. This was a bad decision on my mother's part since age restrictions were in effect, and the film was *verboten* to anyone under the age of fourteen. I was not even twelve and I'm sure I looked even younger.

Mama got our tickets, and I slipped into the cinema unnoticed just as the movie started. I think my mother planned it that way, assuming that nobody would pay attention to us as we entered the darkened theater. Unfortunately, she was mistaken. Just as we were about to sit down, a policeman spotted me. He accosted my mother and asked both of us to step outside into the lobby of the movie theatre.

"How old is this child?" he demanded of my mother.

She didn't lie.

He said, "Do you know that this movie is restricted? Under fourteen years of age, *verboten*."

The next thing he asked was our name and exact address. Again, my mother did not lie. She gave our actual address.

By the time we got home, Mama was in a panic. She told Maxi what had happened. He was incredulous that Mama had taken such an inexplicable risk. We all knew the consequences if the police followed up by coming to the address that Mama had given them. She would be interrogated—so would we all—and there was no saying what the authorities would decide to do. We always lived with the fear we would be discovered and deported. However slight this infraction, it could be the mistake that finished us.

Mama, or perhaps Maxi, decided that we needed help from the Oel family. Superintendents of the building across from us, the Oels were known party members and wore their party pins all the time. Frau Oel was a neighborhood gossip. From a perch at the second-floor window of her building, she kept constant surveillance over street activities and helped cultivate rumors. My mother reasoned that, if properly bribed, the Oels might be able to intercede in our favor. And there was a real possibility the Oels would be sympathetic. Many times, Mama won sympathy from people who realized the difficulties she faced, raising three children on her own without a husband. Given that Frau Oel had a family of her own and, like us, faced the day-to-day challenges of living in a war-stricken city, perhaps her sense of Party loyalty would be outweighed by empathy. Or so Mama hoped.

Of course, in approaching any neighbor with a request, it helped to give something in exchange. While I'm not sure what food gifts Mama brought to the Oels, I am sure she did not approach her empty-handed. In any case, Frau Oel did listen to her story and afterward did her best to set Mama's mind at ease. Frau Oel was sure the police would never pay further attention. They had achieved their purpose by scaring us. Besides, we had not even seen the whole movie because Mama and I had to leave right in the beginning. By now, Frau Oel was sure, Mama's name and address had already been lost among the files.

Her words were reassuring, but I don't think Mama, Maxi, Lilly, or I really believed Frau Oel. The incident only heightened our fear that someday soon there would come the knock on the door. For weeks afterward, that expectation hung over us day and night. As Max remembers it, "Terrible suspense in the next days and weeks! It won't stop at the question of censure for minors; inevitably they will discover that Käthe was not only a minor, but—according to Nuremberg racial laws—also Jewish. And what will happen then . . . ?"

Mama made sure she had all our proper documents handy, and she double-checked the clothes hanging in our closets to make sure all the yellow stars were properly sewn in place.

As it turned out, Frau Oel was right. The police never came.

CHAPTER 16

Air Raids—the Catacombs

M AX KEPT TRACK OF THE POLITICAL HAPPENINGS: "Stalingrad—the war seems to take a different course. The German successes seem to come to an end and new hope arises. . . . The war will not be won by the Nazis and all the Jewish people in Europe will survive! Let us hope so. . . . We listen to our neighbor's radio secretly to hear news from BBC—London—it gives us hope and strength!

"A turning point in the course of the war: Stalingrad! El Alamein! The Nazi war machine suffers its first great defeats; we again begin to hope. . . . For the time being life goes on as always. The illusion of a 'normal life' in that ground-floor dwelling continues."

• • • • •

Had we believed just what we read in the newspapers, we would have thought Hitler's army was invincible. We did have other sources, however, and from them we began to see chinks in the Nazi armor. During fall and winter of late 1942 and early 1943, we heard that the Nazi drive into Russia had been halted. The word "Stalingrad" was mentioned again and again. To me this was no more than a distant city in a part of the world colder than Vienna (if that was imaginable). The Russians in Stalingrad had, at last, resisted the inexorable advance of German forces. I don't think I had ever met a real Russian, and had only the sketchiest knowledge of that distant country, but I knew the Russian army was on the side of the Allies and that's what counted for us. If Stalingrad did not fall, there was hope for all of us. The adults I overheard seemed to think that a Russian victory over Hitler could lead to a decisive change in the war. They frequently reminded one another that "not even Napoleon could conquer Russia in the winter . . . and the Germans can't either."

Through those long winter months when the words "Russia" and "Stalingrad" hung in the air, I had no real understanding of the devastation, the mass starvation, or the street-by-street battles that were being fought by the desperate Russian people. But by December, Maxi and Mama were saying the German army had been surrounded. Hitler had failed in a last-ditch effort to break through the Russian lines and save the hundreds of thousands of German troops trapped by the Red army. In what must have been late January or early February of 1943, I was aware that the Russian army had triumphed; the Germans on the Eastern front were defeated. I may not have quite understood what adults were saying about the Eastern or Western fronts, but at last it seemed like the end of war could be in sight. (That, I *certainly* understood!) Perhaps it would not be so long before some army (we assumed it would be the Russians) pushed the Germans out of

Austria and liberated Vienna. Always, no matter what the news or rumors, we clung to the hope that we would survive this war and someday be free.

But a summer had to pass, followed by another terrible winter, before we heard the news that—we felt with absolute certainty—truly spelled the end for Hitler. The successful Normandy invasion by Allied troops in June of 1944 was followed by a stream of reports saying British and American forces were moving steadily in our direction across western Europe.

The war was at our doorstep. Hopes soared when we heard that Russian troops had entered Hungary. The Hungarian people were celebrating liberation! Then came news that made our spirits plunge. The Germans had thrown back the advancing Russian forces and retaken Budapest. The Nazi victory was followed by mass executions of Hungarian citizens, meted out as punishment for those who had celebrated too early. We were hoping that this would not happen to Vienna and resolved that we would be more careful in our spontaneous rejoicing than the Hungarians had been. When the Russians came to Vienna—and we were almost certain they would—there would be no early celebrations.

Meanwhile, in Vienna we saw visible signs that the Nazis were prepared to mount a strong defense. Most prominent were the *Flakturm*, the specially built towers mounted with antiaircraft guns. In months to come, the harsh rattle of these weapons would become a familiar sound.

This was a time of incredible stress for us. We were living in a constant state of fear and uncertainty, ever afraid of the outcome of the unpredictable and dangerous life we were living. We lived in a place between shadow and light, having an obstructed view of our world, not knowing what the next day might bring. Naturally this stress was made manifest in occasional quarrels and bickering, but we always tried to remember that our strength lay in our unity—our family.

$$\bullet \ \bullet \ \bullet \ \bullet \ \bullet$$

We learned to respond instantly to the howl of air-raid sirens. A first warning meant Allied bombers were approaching the city. We were to head immediately to the nearest air-raid shelter. If Maxi was at work when the siren sounded, it was just Mama, Lilly, and I joining the throngs racing toward the catacombs many blocks away in the inner city, the *Seitenstettengasse*, the oldest section of Vienna. These deep tunnels, far below street level, were said to have been built by the Turks centuries before. Crammed in a sea of moving bodies, holding tightly to Mama and Lilly's hands, I was hemmed in on all sides as we began the steep descent through the stairs and tunnels of the ancient labyrinth. The wail of a second alarm added urgency to our steps, and there were times when I feared being crushed in the mass of people pressing forward.

In the melee making its way down into the bomb shelters, no one ever voiced suspicion that we were Jewish. In fact, most people out of the Second District did not even suspect there were Jews among them. We moved with the crowd like anyone else. But even at moments like these, we told ourselves: *We must act like them! We must not attract attention!*

Once in the depths of the catacombs, there was no place to sit—and scarcely any room to move. Accompanied by coughs, whispers, and murmuring voices, we held our places, attentive and immobilized, faces illuminated by the small dim electric bulbs that lined the arched stone ceiling.

Finally there was motion again as, far above our heads, the all-clear siren sounded and the tense crowd began to reverse its journey. It wasn't until we reached the streets that I felt I could breathe again. (To this day I suffer from claustrophobia and cannot bear to be trapped in a crowded or closed area.)

As raids became more frequent, intervals between first and second warnings were sometimes so brief we had no time to get to the catacombs. Instead, we descended into our own cellar. There, at least, I was surrounded by the familiar faces of our neighbors with their children.

But in some ways, our cellar was worse than the catacombs. Under bombardment the cellar offered minimal protection. In the catacombs I never felt anything more than a slight shudder of earth when bombs fell. But in the cellar of Herminengasse 15, with nothing more than wooden floorboards overhead to protect us from the thunderous noise, any nearby explosion felt like a direct hit. The building shuddered, dust rained down. The noise was a physical sensation like a body blow. At the worst moments—one bomb exploded less than a hundred meters away—I was certain our building would come crashing down on top of us. By the time the all-clear siren sounded and we could stagger up from the cellar, I was scarcely conscious. As we stumbled up the stairs and returned to our apartment, I felt shaken and breathless from fear. Mother and Lilly were wrecks as well.

It was during one of these raids that we lost our goldfish. There were two goldfish that had lived for two years in a small tank that stood on the ledge of the kitchen window facing the courtyard. Each day I would talk to them as I poured the powdered fish food into their tank. Emerging from the basement after one of those nerve-wracking raids, I was horrified to see that the kitchen window had crashed and shattered, spilling broken glass over the sill and into the tank. The little tank was intact, but either the vibration of the bombings or the shards of window glass had ended the lives of our goldfish. The sight of their small floating bodies made me very sad. Perhaps the goldfish reminded me of our family, trapped in a small world, literally and figuratively, unable to be free beyond our confines. I hoped their same sad fate would not befall us.

But our family was lucky. On one of those occasions when we did not have enough warning and had to hide in the cellar, the catacombs got a direct hit. A bomb must have streaked in at an angle, penetrating the entrance, landing inside the chambers. The detonation spread havoc through sealed tunnels. Many people were killed—among them, one of our friends who worked with our protector.

CHAPTER 17

Dangerous Train Rides

DESPITE THE ONSET OF ALLIED BOMBINGS, TRAINS and buses continued to run. Mama and I kept up our visits to the country, taking clothing and city goods available to us for our relatives and returning with food to tide us over coming weeks. But as the war continued, it became less and less safe to travel.

On one of our journeys, we were accosted by people we thought were Yugoslav partisans. Previous to this particular journey, we had heard that partisans would sometimes appear on trains and rob people of their jewelry and money. Then, one day, we witnessed firsthand what was happening. Mama and I were headed to the country and riding in a railcar with just a few passengers when we suddenly became aware of a commotion in the back of the car. I turned to see two handsome young men, both brandishing knives, making their way forward through the car, threatening passengers and commanding them to hand over any jewelry they were wearing and money they were carrying. These men wore no uniforms, carried no guns.

Mother and I looked all around, hoping a train conductor or guard would come to the rescue. There was no one to be seen. The young men approaching us moved swiftly from one passenger to the next. When I heard them speak, it was in a guttural language that was certainly not German. It vaguely resembled the Croatian that my mother spoke when she was with our country relatives.

In other circumstances we might have regarded these partisans as our friends. Like us, they hated Hitler and his army. They worked as an underground organization. We regarded them as fearless resistance fighters. In their own country they had constantly attempted to sabotage the Nazi regime. Many of them had lost their lives doing heroic work. They had our admiration.

What they were doing now made no sense to us. Obviously, they needed money to maintain their struggle. But why had they crossed the border to prey on Austrian civilians? Why did they take such a risk?

When it was finally our turn, one of the partisans noticed the wedding ring on my mother's finger. A struggle ensued as he started to try to yank it off. It was too tight. I had horrible thoughts. *What if the man cuts off Mama's finger to get the ring?* Mama pleaded with him in a voice that was inaudible to the other passengers. Since Mama was speaking Croatian, I didn't know exactly what she was saying to the partisan as he pulled at the ring on her finger. And while her words alone might have convinced them, I think once again my appearance as a gaunt and skinny-looking child played in our favor. Whatever their reason, they gave up the struggle for Mama's ring, ignored our rucksacks, rapidly moved on, and in no time at all jumped off the train.

Throughout all this, the train never stopped moving. We saw no conductors or guards during the rest of the journey. It seemed inexplicable that no one interfered with their actions. Once the partisans were gone, the passengers complained fiercely. They were horrified that no one had come to the rescue.

To this day I do not know why the partisans were able to act with apparent impunity in preying on travelers. They regarded all Austrians—even civilians—as complicit with the Germans. I'm quite sure it helped that my mother spoke Croatian. Even if they had not understood every word of her plea, they had to know we were victims—as they were—of the Nazi regime. As for the whispered revelation—whatever it was—I have no idea whether that too weighed in our favor. We later learned that the train crew themselves were held hostage while the episode ensued.

• • • • •

An equally terrifying train episode occurred a short time afterward.

In addition to razing the city with bombers, the Allies used strafing planes (I heard them called *Tiefflieger*) to target moving trains. The planes attacked with machine guns. Their tactic was to swoop low over a train and pepper the cars with rapid fire. Munitions transports were probably equipped with antiaircraft guns for defense, but the passenger train Mama and I traveled on had no such protection.

I don't know which came first—the sound of the *Tiefflieger* or the rattle of machine-gun fire—but suddenly the train had stopped and passengers all around us were screaming. Plane engines roared and the clatter of machine guns filled our ears as we scrambled to escape.

I have no idea how we got out. Through open doors or shattered windows? All I remember is tumbling out of the train and lying flat on the embankment.

It was over in minutes. The rattle of bullets ceased, the thunder of aircraft died away. Mama and I lay on the ground beside each other, dazed, dirty, shaken but alive.

We must have climbed back on the train. We must have resumed our journey home. Perhaps there was wreckage in the railway car—passengers crying, people wounded. I don't remember. All I know is, Mama and I survived.

We would not ride the train again or see our relatives in the country until the war had ended. Even if Mama had decided to leave me behind and travel by herself by some other means, the trip would have been too dangerous.

Somehow, we would have to get by on the food reserves we still had in Vienna. And they were dwindling rapidly.

CHAPTER 18

The SS in Our Cellar

DURING THE LAST SEVEN DAYS OF THE WAR, THE cellar of Herminengasse 15 was our last refuge. It became home for my family and for most of the other residents of the building.

At the bottom of the cellar stairs to the right side was an open area with an earth floor. This became a common room. Each resident in the building had been assigned a small cubicle with a door, measuring about eight by ten feet, where they stored coal or wood. When the shelling and crossfire got so bad that we could no longer stay in the apartment, we moved to the cellar, and these cubicles became our sleeping and living rooms.

Ours was just to the left at the bottom of the stairway. Max took apart Lilly's cast-iron bed and brought it down into our cubicle, where he reassembled it. We were supposed to take turns resting or, if possible, sleeping on this one bed. It took up most of the space in the cubicle. There was no light from the outdoors. We had petroleum lamps, and we kept them lit at all times in case we had to evacuate to the upstairs quickly—but always on low, to prevent the glass from getting smoky and to avoid permeating the air with petroleum smell. (I am sure this was a fire hazard, and could have been disastrous if we had been hit by a bomb, but no one said anything.)

As few times as I had visited the cellar to fetch coal, I had never imagined that anyone could live down there for even a short time. I understood why we had to stay down there; at the age of thirteen I was grown up enough to know there was now no alternative. Our apartment was no longer safe.

Nearly everyone still living in the building sought sanctuary in the cellar during the final days. There was the blond, somewhat rough-looking veteran soldier, Herr Kopica, who, because of his war wounds, had been largely housebound throughout most of the last years of the war. Alongside him was his wife, the tall, dark-haired Frau Kopica in her housedress, and the children whom Lilly and I had so often played with—Ditta, Isa, and Franzi. I watched Frau Bruckner, sour-faced as always, come down the cellar stairs leading her deaf husband, hunched over his cane. As our life in the cellar began to settle into a routine, Frau Bruckner seemed to spend most of her time lurking around the aisle, apparently keeping her eyes on the rest of us, especially Frau Sidie. Herr Bruckner kept to their cubicle.

And there was Frau Sidie—looking calm, secure, and lovely as ever. Her handsome partner, Herr Fritz, could often be seen in the dim light strolling restlessly up and down the aisle, while their son, Willie, sat in their cubicle.

Willie's health had deteriorated during the war. He had contracted polio and was hospitalized for quite a while. (Though he would eventually recover from the most severe effects, I believe one side of his body might still be afflicted as it seems he has limited control over one arm and hand.) What drew him out of the cubicle at regular intervals was the need to take care of Chippie, their dog. The family knew they could not bring Chippie down to the cellar, but this meant at regular intervals Willie had to climb out of the cellar and ascend the three flights up to his family's apartment bearing scraps of food for his pet. (Chippie's usual necessary walks outdoors must have been limited during this time.)

Occupying another cubicle were Frau Freisl and her chubby, nine-year-old daughter, Fanny. Frau Freisl was relatively new to our building and had moved in a number of years after the deportation. She looked far too old to have such a young daughter; in an earlier conversation with Frau Freisl, my mother had learned that Fanny was in fact adopted. Frau Freisl explained that she had twelve sons of her own, but had always wanted a daughter, and when she realized it just was not going to happen, she took the initiative of adopting a girl. Fanny kept close to her mother. She was well behaved, acted very grown up for her age, and it looked like she already took good care of Frau Freisl.

A number of our neighbors never appeared in the cellar. The Churans, our neighbors, had fled to another district with their children, Helli and Karli. Since Herr Churan was gentile, he must have concluded their chances were better if they stayed with his gentile family, who lived in another district of Vienna.

Also absent was Frau Bergman, the trembling old lady who was so fond of cats. She never came down from her top-floor apartment to join us. Though we never found out the reason, it would be typical of her not to bother; she simply did not care about life and accepted her fate.

The other missing person was our building superintendent, Herr Vicecka. He may have sought shelter in the cellar of his carpentry workshop, or possibly he moved to the cellar of one of his girlfriends.

The Hecht family—Erna, Frau, and Herr Hecht—who lived in the same apartment as Frau Sidie, stayed quietly in their cellar cubicle but mingled in the common room when the shooting and bombing would quiet down for a little while.

• • • • •

During the entire seven days we were in the cellar, my mother appeared to be calm, although I knew she did not feel this way. During an earlier bombing raid when we had been forced to run to the cellar, I had been terrified when Mama went into hysterics. As the building shook from the bomb blasts, she fell to her knees, clutching at Max, Lilly, and I, screaming, "Oh my God! Oh my God! We're going to die!" Her panic had set off a chain reaction. Some of the children—much younger than we were—began to become restless and cry. After the shelling stopped, Frau Kopica had taken Max aside and said to my brother, "You must tell your mother she can't do that. She frightens the children too much. If she goes into hysterics again, we cannot allow her to stay down here with us and the children."

That was enough. Whatever Mama's fear of the bombs, her terror at the prospect of being evicted—with all of us—was even greater.

• • • • •

Looking back, recalling the feelings of a wide-eyed, thirteen-year-old girl in the cellar, I remember unending terror. This had to be the end of the war. But what did that mean? The bombing and artillery fire could not go on forever. There had to be a way out of that place—a future time when the noise, fire, and destruction would stop. But would I live through this? At any moment, one of those bombs could come through the ceiling, and that would be the end of all of us.

The noise was incredible. Bombings and shootings never ceased. It seemed certain that this cellar, our final refuge, could be the place where we all died. It was impossible to sleep. (During the long days and nights, even resting on the bed, we were always fully dressed, ready to run at any moment in case a bomb hit our building.) I might have dozed off now and then out of exhaustion, but with the crash of a bomb or the rattle of artillery, I would be shocked into full alertness and lie there with my eyes wide open, staring at the dim, quivering glow of the flame of the petroleum lamp.

The concept of dying was something my young mind previously envisioned as being for old people, something very far away from me. At this time, though, I think I felt the fear that it might happen sooner. But I also felt that if I could somehow live through this, I would live forever.

• • • • •

Despite the nearly constant battle in the streets, there were times when we had to go out for water. Early on during the shelling, the main pipes leading to the house were destroyed. Faucets stopped working. We couldn't flush our toilet. The nearest source of water was a fire hydrant more than a ten-minute walk from our building.

In the beginning, during lulls in the fighting, Lilly and I took up pitchers, Mama and Maxi carried pails, and we made our way through the streets to join the crowds around the open hydrant. We filled our containers to the top and tried to spill as little as possible as we trudged back to the building and downstairs to the cellar. It might be many days before we could safely step into the street again.

A portion of fresh water was set aside for cooking and washing dishes. The rest was for our own needs. In our cubicle of the cellar, we had one *lavoir* and a pail. The *lavoir* was for washing up, and the pail held the dirty water that we saved after spritzing ourselves. Even this was not wasted. When I had to use the toilet, I waited for a lull in the shooting and made my way upstairs carrying the pail of dirty water. Hurriedly, I used the toilet, poured water from the pail into the toilet bowl to make it flush, then raced down to the cellar again.

Though both Lilly and I had often played with the young children in our building, once in the cellar I cannot recall a single moment when we attempted to distract them with games or lessons. I think we were all too scared to think of anything but our own families. Ditta, Isa, and Franzi Kopica all clung to their parents. As for Lilly and me, we wanted to stay close to Max and Mama, fearing most of all that we might be separated if a bomb hit.

Even before we went down to the cellar, all our families had been subsisting on very little food. Our reserves were so depleted that we had little more than flour and pig's fat. These were often the only ingredients of our meals.

Frau and Herr Kopica brought down a one-burner cooking stove or heater, fueled by petroleum, that they used for food preparation. For meals, Frau Kopica mixed the flour with water to create dough that she flattened into a round shape. My mother contributed our household's remaining supply of pig's fat. Cooking over a single blue flame, Frau Kopica fried the dough in the pig's fat and then handed it to the children.

· · · · ·

Through those days, shelling, bombing, and machine-gun fire built to a crescendo until there was a continuous roar overhead. Sounds were impossible to interpret. I could only guess where a bomb had struck or a building had come crashing down. Everything felt like it was happening directly above our heads.

One thing I knew for sure. The Nazis were fighting back. Otherwise, this would all be over. From what I had heard on the Churans' radio before they left, I knew the Reich had fallen. The Allies were going to win. Russian troops were on the verge of liberating Vienna. But the Nazis were not finished.

And then we heard that, even in the final hours of the war, the Nazis were executing Jews.

The information came from Frau and Herr Zellner, who had fled from their apartment in the Foerstergasse, also in the ghetto (Second *Bezirk*), a few minutes from our house. The Zellners were scrambling from house to house and cellar to cellar. No one in our building recognized them. They were just two strangers who suddenly appeared. They literally crawled into our cellar, scrambling through a hole that led from an adjacent cellar. Theirs had been a panicked flight from the Foestergasse. There, they said, Nazis were clearing out Jews, lining them against the walls, and shooting them. Sadly enough we came to find out they spoke the truth.

(After the war, a memorial was erected in the Jewish cemetery, dedicated to nine Jewish people who had been executed one day before the liberation of Vienna. Just as the Zellners described, the SS had ordered all Jews out from one particular building, lined them up facing the wall, and executed them. The memorial, which bears the names of all nine victims, has the inscription "Here laid to rest are nine Martyrs murdered by Nazi-henchmen on April 12, 1945, shortly before liberation.")

Adding to the threat of bombs and artillery, we now had this to fear—execution by firing squad.

As Frau and Herr Zellner told us what they had seen, they pleaded that we allow them to stay in our improvised bomb shelter. I remember the people in our cellar were hesitant since it meant another two mouths to feed, but fortunately for the Zellners they had not come empty handed. The food they carried was the most precious commodity imaginable—real meat. At last, we would have some relief from our diet of water, flour, and pig's fat. The little cooker was fired up, and Frau Kopica prepared a meat goulash. The Zellners were welcome to stay.

•　•　•　•　•

As the days and nights dragged on, none of us could ignore the conflict building between Frau Bruckner and Frau Sidie. Everyone said Frau Bruckner was simply jealous. Young as I was, I could see many reasons why a gaunt-looking, bad-tempered, childless person like her would be resentful of Frau Sidie, a woman who (in my eyes) was so attractive, good-natured, and gracious. To me it was no contest: I favored Frau Sidie. Frau Bruckner seemed mean and vindictive. Frau Sidie was well liked by our building residents and this only fueled Frau Bruckner's detestation. But there may have been other factors as well. Frau Sidie lived with Herr Fritz and Willie in an apartment on the third floor that Frau Bruckner coveted. She knew that Frau Sidie was Jewish and that she and Herr Fritz were not married, yet this couple had an apartment that was better than hers! Adding fuel to the fire, I also heard that Frau Bruckner objected to Chippie, Willie's fox terrier, who sometimes barked.

Whatever its exact source, Frau Bruckner's jealousy was no secret. Now, forced to live side by side with Frau Sidie in the cellar, Frau Bruckner's vindictive attacks grew steadily worse. I can't recall how Frau Sidie defended herself, or even if she did I believe she tried to ignore it to avoid any argument. (Being Jewish, we were fearful of everything at all times; we did not want to make "much noise" about anything—and certainly not draw the attention of others who might find a reason to get rid of us.)

At last, Frau Bruckner's attacks reached a level that no one could ignore. Finally Herr Fritz—so often pacing back and forth—came to a halt before Frau Bruckner and confronted her. He told her in no uncertain terms that when the city fell into Allied hands, he would see that she met her punishment.

"They will be here soon," Herr Fritz told the woman. "You will never again be able to threaten my wife. I will make sure of that."

I don't recall Frau Bruckner's response. But it was just a short time afterward that she announced, "I'm going to fetch water; I have to get some water for my husband." She picked up a pitcher and headed out of the cellar.

We thought she had lost her mind. The shelling had become constant. No one was safe in the streets. Further, Frau Bruckner was not the type of person who would risk her life to fetch water. Why had she suddenly gone on this suicide mission? Everyone was surprised and wondering but no one cared enough to hold her back. (Her husband probably thought nothing of his wife going for water since he was too deaf to hear the shelling and crossfire.)

She went no farther than the nearest police station, which was run by the SS. There, she reported that a Jewish woman, Frau Sidie, was hiding in the cellar of a building in Herminengasse 15. Frau Sidie, she said, was looking forward to the "liberation" with all her heart. She couldn't wait for the Russians to take Vienna and finish the German army. If the officers would just follow her, she would prove it to them.

We knew none of this at the time, of course, but there was a clamor in the street when Frau Bruckner returned with four or five SS officers. Suddenly, the front door of our building was being hammered with a violent barrage of rifle butts.

Mama's reaction was instantaneous. She called Maxi out of the cellar and told him to jump over the wall of the courtyard into the next building's yard where he could make a run for it. (We all knew that if the Gestapo found a military-age young man hiding out, he would be seized immediately and possibly shot for not being in the army or for being Jewish.) Maxi dashed from the cellar and leapt over the wall. Instantly there was the sound of gunfire, and he was back. Whatever his chances in the cellar, they were better than on the street where he was sure to be caught in the crossfire.

By the time the soldiers got to the head of the cellar stairway, Max was already down in the farthest corner of our dark cubicle. Mama and Lilly stood in front of it so Maxi could not be seen. As long as the SS did not closely search the entire cellar, there was a chance he would go undetected.

As for Frau Bruckner, all her venom was now directed on her rival as she led the uniformed men down the stairs.

"There!" she declared, pointing at Frau Sidie. "That's the woman I told you about. She's a Jew. She said she can't wait for the Russians to come."

One of the soldiers stepped up to Frau Sidie. He swung his rifle against the side of her head. Blood spurted from a gash in her cheek as she fell to the floor.

Triumphant, Frau Bruckner now pointed to Willie. "That is her son!" Then she turned on Herr Fritz. "This is *the boy's father*. But he is not her husband!"

Up to then, it was as if everyone was in shock except Herr Kopica. He stepped forward, confronting the SS soldiers to speak in defense of Frau Sidie, Herr Fritz, and Willie. As Herr Kopica was dealing with the soldiers in the cellar, I made my way to the top of the stairs where a single young man in an SS uniform had been posted as guard, with rifle ready. He could not have been older than our Max, perhaps about twenty. For some reason (I still can't understand where this impulse came from), I looked up at him and asked, in my childish voice, "Do you have a candy?"

What he saw at that moment was a skinny little girl with big brown eyes. My innocent words had the desired effect. He lowered his gun. "No, we don't get candy." I did not know what else to say to him. All I knew was, my words had distracted him and that was what I hoped for. I do not know what exactly was going on in him, but his face began to have a different look, much softer.

Down in the cellar, the soldiers kept to their mission. They were preparing to take Frau Sidie, Herr Fritz, and Willie with them. What would these soldiers do to them? Maybe if I made friends with this one soldier, he would be the one to let them all go. Could this be what I was thinking?

I have no idea. But my little ploy—the plea for candy—had made that soldier lower his weapon. For the moment, that was all that mattered.

At the very time that I was making my bold, childish request for candy, the SS seized Frau Sidie and her family. Herr Kopica stepped forward and volunteered to go with them, wherever they were being taken. In the hours that followed, I would later learn, he exercised his influence on their behalf. Among all those in our building, Herr Kopica was the only one the soldiers would possibly listen to. It was he, after all, who had fought on Hitler's side in the war. He was a wounded veteran. Most of his brothers and brothers-in-law fought for Hitler and were possibly in the SS themselves.

His words counted. When he insisted that this was nothing but the revenge of a jealous woman—that there was absolutely no reason to hold Frau Sidie and her family hostage in this petty dispute—he must have caught the ear of the officer who decided these matters. Or maybe the attentive officer knew this was the end of the war, and that perhaps he would need someone to stand up for him very soon. It could not be much longer before these officers themselves might stand before the Allied authorities if they survived.

As for those of us remaining in the basement, we were frozen with the terror of not knowing what was to come next. The SS knew where we were now. And we were acutely aware of what the Zellners had told us about the executions in the Foerstergasse.

How exactly Herr Kopica did it, I'll never know—but soon he was back among us, and with him came Frau Sidie, Herr Fritz, and Willie. Frau Sidie held a napkin against her swollen bloody cheek where the SS's gun had hit her. Herr Kopica, apparently, had continued to insist it was nothing more than a domestic dispute among two women, and his influence had prevailed. He did not think the SS would bother us again.

Frau Bruckner did not reappear. She must have made arrangements for her husband, because someone came to lead Herr Bruckner up the stairs and out of the cellar.

We surmised that Herr Bruckner had joined his wife in finding another cellar where they would be taken in. All I know is, for the remainder of our hours in the cellar, we neither saw them nor heard from them again. And in spite of the reassurance of Herr Kopica, we did not rest until it was all over, constantly thinking of the tragedy in the Foerstergasse just one day before the liberation.

(There was, however, one last sighting of Frau Bruckner, shortly after the liberation, when she returned to the cellar to collect her belongings. Eventually, Herr Fritz saw to it that she was arrested and went to trial. At the trial, Max was the star witness and, once under oath, had to admit to the judge that Herr Fritz had as much as told Frau Bruckner that he would report her to the Russians as soon as the war was over. This was interpreted as a threat and therefore Frau Bruckner received a prison sentence of six weeks, which everyone thought was very little considering that all the Jews in our building could have been shot like those in the Foerstergasse.)

CHAPTER 19

The Final Hours

O N OUR SEVENTH DAY IN THE CELLAR, IT SEEMED at last there was a lull in the fighting. The intervals lengthened between each of the shattering explosions. The roar of artillery seemed more distant.

When would it be safe to leave the cellar? No one knew for sure. By now I was far too exhausted to pay attention. For days all I had wanted to do was sleep—really sleep—without being shocked awake by shell fire. At last it seemed as if that might be possible. Oblivious to everything but my need to rest, I crawled into the big cast-iron bed that Mama and Max had placed in our cubicle. My eyes closed. For the first time in what seemed like an eternity, I drifted into a state resembling unconsciousness.

I don't know what finally woke me. Perhaps it was the absolute absence of noise. When I opened my eyes at last, I found myself enveloped in still darkness. The petroleum lamps were not lit. Suddenly disoriented, I panicked.

I could see nothing, hear no one. My mind raced. The Nazis had come while I slept, rounded up everyone, and taken them away! Everyone had been killed while I slept.

"Mama! Mama! Mama!" I don't know how many times I shouted for her. Did I whimper or scream? The only response to my desperate cries was a deep silence that could mean only one thing. Everyone was gone. I was alone.

I tried to clamber out of the bed. Where was I? I could not get oriented from my deep sleep and the darkness in the cellar cubicle. Why was the petroleum lamp not lit? Where was the door? I put my naked feet down at last and, to my relief, felt the familiar dirt. But which way was I facing? I couldn't tell. I took a step and suddenly I was up to the ankle in cold water. At the same moment, there was a familiar sound of tin against earth. I realized what I had done. I had stepped into the water-filled pail that was always positioned near the foot of the bed.

Now I was oriented. The door was just a few steps away on the opposite side. I moved in that direction, pressed with my hand, and sure enough, the door swung open. There was no break in the darkness, but now, at least, I knew where I was—at the very foot of the stairs. Still listening, with a stealth inspired by abject terror, I made my way step by step up the stairs to the lobby barefoot.

I heard voices—high-pitched shouting, almost delirious. And then the words, suddenly intelligible, "We are free! We are free! The Russians are here!"

I rushed out. Max, Mama, and Lilly were all outside in the front of our building among the throngs crowding the street. People were shouting at the top of their lungs, literally leaping in celebration. There were hugs, tears, bursts of laughter. In an instant, I was infected by the delirious joy. This was liberation at last! I have never forgotten the feelings of relief I felt as a thirteen-year-old girl.

I saw uniforms I had never seen before—Russian soldiers in the streets. Tanks rumbled past. I held out my hands as the Russians tossed parcels of food to us.

Then I knew what had happened. Of course my family had not forgotten me. They were just so happy that their youngest finally got a night's sleep that they had decided not to awaken me.

In all the excitement, my recent moments of terror simply evaporated. We were out of the cellar—out of the darkness—at last, and for good.

Others, I know, issued cautious reminders even in the midst of celebration. We couldn't forget what had happened during the Hungarian "liberation"—how the Germans had returned even after the Russians took Budapest. It may have taken hours, even days, before we could truly accept that the Germans were irreversibly defeated.

And yet it seemed to be true: the war was finally over. I discovered later that at the war's end only 619 Jews remained in Vienna.† Mama, Max, Lilly, and I would be among them.

---

† Moser, Museum of Tolerance online.

CHAPTER 20

Liberated—April 1945

THE STREETS OF VIENNA LOOKED AS IF A MASSIVE act of vandalism had been perpetrated. Most buildings in our district were still standing, but many were bombed out and nearly all had been riddled with shells. On those that remained, exteriors were pockmarked, windows gone.

Our apartment was intact. What we needed most desperately was food. Others were in the same desperate straits. Meanwhile, there was rampant plundering by Russian troops.

We heard a rumor that a bakery had been overtaken by starving people who were taking away sacks of flour, and Max managed to get to the bakery before it was stripped bare. The one sack of flour Maxi managed to carry home from the bakery on his back was what saved us from starvation. Later, when stores started to reopen, we found that you could bring one kilo of flour to the bakery in exchange for a loaf of bread with only the cost of baking to pay for. We treasured that one sack of flour and tried to make it last as long as possible.

In the weeks that followed, bread and coffee comprised most of our meals. There was no milk. That sack of flour proved to be an incredible life saver.

As for meat, the only kind available was horsemeat. Horses that had been killed in the final battle lay where they had fallen in streets and parks. Those most desperately hungry butchered them where they lay. Eventually, you could also buy stringy horsemeat at butcher shops, though we all suspected the butchers acquired their meat the same way—from the fallen horses lying in streets and parks. It was impossible to say exactly what the butchers were offering in those days.

Given all the bombed-out and uninhabitable buildings, there was an immediate apartment shortage. Jewish families were to be given preference, however, as apartments became available, and some were able to move quickly. Frau Sidie, Herr Fritz, and Willie soon moved into a large apartment in the Ninth District, a very residential area of Vienna.

Meanwhile, surviving Jews from other countries were pouring into Vienna with the expectation that they would only be living there temporarily while they were waiting for immigration visas. Among the countries accepting Austrians were the United States, Canada, and Australia. But there were quotas.

The Churans were the first ones emigrating to England, where part of her family fled before the war. We unfortunately lost contact with them, for which I am truly sorry.

We applied for immigration papers that would allow us to join our relatives in New York. But we recognized that it could be years before our quota would become due. Despite being considered Holocaust survivors, we were still recognized as Austrian citizens and the Austrian quota was very low. In the meantime we had to focus on survival. At war's end, in addition to the scarcity of food, no one could find jobs or apartments. True, we were not as bad off as the Jewish refugees from other countries, who had to be accommodated in hospitals and other institutions because of lack of living quarters. At least we still had our own place to live in. But it was not where we intended to stay. It had been a war refuge for us—a place where we hoped to survive but not a place to continue with our lives. And it was obvious we could not subsist forever on bread and coffee.

• • • • •

In the immediate aftermath of the liberation, we had to accept the fact that the Russian presence had to be dealt with in nearly every aspect of our daily lives. We were grateful to them for being liberators—that was something we would not forget—but we soon became aware that the soldiers were not necessarily our friends. They treated Jews no different from other citizens, but, since Austrian soldiers had fought on the side of Germany, they viewed all Austrians as their recent enemies. There were tales of rampant pillaging, plundering, and raping.

The Russians, however, had access to a precious commodity they were sometimes willing to barter—food. The items they most desired in exchange were watches. In certain black market areas, especially around the *Schwarzenbergplatz,* were Russian soldiers hanging about who were looking to buy watches and other goods. Unrestricted trade went on in other parts of the city as well. Approaching citizens and asking for *"Ura, Ura"* (the Russian pronunciation of the German word *uhr,* for watch), they would sometimes offer food in exchange.

CHAPTER 21

Frau Sidie

FRAU SIDIE WAS FORTUNATE IN ONE TRADE, THOUGH the transaction initially looked like folly on her part. Constantly on the lookout for food, one day she sighted a Russian soldier who she thought appeared to be Jewish walking alongside a number of other soldiers. Acting on impulse, she approached the man and showed him her valuable watch, saying in Russian, "We need food. If you can bring me some food, I will give you this *'ura.'*" She was a daring and courageous woman! How could she possibly have trusted this Russian soldier at first sight?

The Russian agreed easily and asked her to give him the watch right away. Tempted by instinct Frau Sidie handed him the watch and also gave him her address to bring her food as an exchange.

When she arrived home I don't know whether Herr Fritz and Willie were astounded or amused by her actions, but they certainly made fun of her gullibility. "You think you will ever see this soldier or your watch again? How could you be so trusting?" Max and my mother, when they heard her story, held the same view. But Frau

Sidie was confident that the soldier was Jewish and would deliver on his promise.

A few days later, there was a hard knock on our building door (which was always kept locked for fear of soldiers coming to the building looking for "*uras*" and women). As we were living on the ground floor, our mother, opening the door cautiously, was greeted by the sight of a Russian soldier who asked for Frau Sidie. His arms were loaded with packages. Mama hailed Frau Sidie to announce that her Russian had indeed arrived with what could be the promised goods.

(The story did not end there, however, and the sequel—as was so often the case with Frau Sidie—added another heroic dimension to her. Subsequent to this visit, Frau Sidie and her family became close friends with this soldier. He was indeed Jewish and his name was Mirtscha. Like so many Russian soldiers who had served in the war, he did not want to go back to Russia—fearing death or imprisonment. The family became very friendly with Mirtscha; he visited them all the time while he was stationed in Vienna. Suddenly, we noticed that he was no longer wearing the Russian uniform but civilian clothes. Mirtscha remained in Vienna and spent a lot of time with Frau Sidie's family until 1956, when the Russian Army ended its occupation of Austria. He was then a free man, no longer a deserter, and was now legally living in Vienna. He never returned to Russia. However, Mirtscha suffered from colon cancer—then incurable. As she had done with others so often before, Frau Sidie devoted much time and care to this former deserter—he had become a part of her family. Mirtscha died at a fairly young age in Vienna.

The family remained this former Russian soldier's best friends to the end of his life.)

• • • • •

Despite such rare exceptions, we generally held that Russian troops were not to be trusted, especially when these war-weary soldiers were in the presence of attractive young women. I observed that special measures had to be taken to protect my eye-catching fifteen-year-old sister, Lilly, and attractive nineteen-year-old Erna Hecht (whose family shared the apartment with the Frau Sidie and her family on the third floor). With Russian soldiers strolling the streets, Mama and Frau Hecht thought it would be best if they hid their daughters in the attic. Of course, it never occurred to me at the time to wonder why I should not also be hidden in the attic, too, but I now understand how unlikely it was that a thin-faced, flat-chested young girl like me would interest even the most libidinous Russian soldier.

In fact, I was totally oblivious. In part, this was because I was simply too innocent. But also, I remember a feeling after the liberation of being quite powerful, as if nothing bad could happen to me ever again. I recall this feeling well, and it lasted quite a while. I walked on the streets with an attitude of "nobody can do anything to me!" (I would even go to those "restricted" movies which—as during the war—were supposedly forbidden to children under the age of fourteen.)

One reason I admired Frau Sidie so much was because she never seemed to fear anything. Only in retrospect have I realized how enormously courageous and daring it was for a beautiful, fair-haired woman like her to venture into the streets while Russian soldiers still had the upper hand, plundering and raping at will. One time when I went with her, I got a glimpse of what risk she was taking.

For anyone bold enough to make a trip to the other side of the river, the warehouses still held many goods that could be of use. They were unlocked—an open invitation to come and take whatever you could. Some were said to be well stocked with clothing. The temptation was great. By now, most of our coats were threadbare, and socks had been so often mended they looked like Swiss cheese.

Frau Sidie said she was ready to go. So was I—and I got no opposition from my family. They fully trusted her judgment.

"Come, Ketl," said Frau Sidie, calling me by my diminutive "little teapot" name, "come with me, and we'll get some clothing for our families."

Following her lead, I made my way with her through the district and over the bridge. Our destination was a warehouse holding the kinds of goods that might be found today in an army-navy store. Its doors had been broken down, and as we approached we saw the upstairs store had already been looted. Then we heard the roar of Russian voices coming up from the basement. Obviously Russian soldiers were down there, and it was easy to guess they were thoroughly drunk.

"Wait here," Frau Sidie cautioned me.

She entered the basement. From my post above and outside, I heard her speaking in Russian. Both her words and the replies of the soldiers were incomprehensible. Almost instantly, it seemed, she returned to my side. Her arms were full, and she was in a great hurry. "Quickly, quickly—we have to *run!*"

We did not stop until we had crossed the bridge and were almost home.

Though a mystery at the time, I am now certain why we had to flee. It would not be hard to imagine the reaction of the Russian soldiers when this beautiful woman appeared like a vision among them. Whatever actions Frau Sidie took and whatever she said to defend herself from the drunken brawlers must have been swift and decisive. Otherwise, I'm sure she would have become yet another victim.

The rewards from that risky expedition were bountiful. When we ran away, Frau Sidie was carrying an entire bag filled with men's socks (which went to Maxi, Herr Fritz, and Willie). For me she had seized what I considered at the time a magnificent loden coat. That coat was a true treasure. It would keep me warm for many winters to come, and my gratitude toward Frau Sidie knew no bounds. How typical of her not to forget me as she was risking herself. Once again, she had demonstrated to me what a bighearted person she truly was.

CHAPTER 22

Walking to Vienna—May 1945

ALL THE WHILE, AS OUR MEAGER FOOD SUPPLIES were diminishing, we were acutely aware that fresh produce was no farther away than our relatives in the country. Certainly there were shortages in the rural areas, but nothing like the virtual famine in Vienna. If we could just get to the family farms, we would certainly find food. But it was impossible to find transportation out of the city. There were no trains, no buses, no cars.

A surprise visit from Aunt Anna, however, reminded us the journey was not unthinkable. She made the sixty-kilometer trip from Antau to Vienna in an oxen cart. When she was ready to return to her village, she invited me to come with her.

My mother agreed instantly. With Aunt Anna I would be well taken care of and would get regular meals. Meanwhile, there would be one less mouth to feed.

I was immediately very excited about this invitation. Riding out from Vienna on Aunt Anna's oxen cart began as another adventure for me. Before we had gone very far, I realized it was going to be a punishing experience. The seat, nothing more than a slab of wood, was an instrument of torture. The cart had no springs, and by the time we had gone a few kilometers, every jolt was like being walloped with a hard paddle. I could hardly complain. But I recall that journey as a brutal test of my endurance. No matter which way I squirmed, I could not get comfortable.

I was hugely relieved to finally arrive at my aunt's house—especially when, for the first time in many weeks, I got to eat my fill of real food from a well-stocked kitchen.

Back in Vienna, Max and Mama realized, whatever the obstacles, they would have to find some way to get to the country. The initial supply of flour that Max had procured was running out. We were down to the last of our bread and coffee. They urgently needed any food that could be spared by our relatives in Antau.

I don't know how, but Max and Mama finally found transportation that would bring them partway to their destination. They walked the rest of the way, making the entire trip to Antau in a single day.

There was a good reason why they made the decision to leave Lilly behind in Vienna. Russian soldiers were all over Eastern Austria, and many of them were in the country. The stories of girls and women being raped by soldiers were not just rumors—as Mama and Maxi well knew—and it would have been dangerous to take Lilly along.

Of course, Mama did not arrive in Antau empty-handed. She brought goods our relatives would surely find of use, items that were more readily available in big cities like Vienna. People in the cities were selling precious things for pennies just to buy scraps of food, so it was easy for mother to acquire such goods cheaply and bring them in to the country in exchange for goods and fresh food available only in the country.

Mama and Max planned to stay just one night to gather provisions before making the return journey together with me. When they arrived at Aunt Anna's, Max settled into the spare house, with Mama and I taking the bedroom in the main house. Our plans were to have a night's rest, then load up a hand-drawn little hand cart and walk back by foot to Vienna.

Mama and I slept that night in the same featherbed that I had previously shared with Aunt Anna. In the middle of the night, I suddenly felt a chill as the cover was yanked off our bed. A Russian soldier had come in while we slept, and now he was staring down at us, a flashlight shining in our eyes. For one paralyzed moment, we looked back at him, helpless. I wondered what he meant to do. Mama, of course, knew.

The next thing I heard was Aunt Anna. She stood in the doorway, speaking rapidly to the soldier in Croatian. A moment passed, then she led the Russian from the room, all the while speaking to him in Croatian.

The next day, nobody said anything. I asked Mama, "What did that soldier want?" She simply said, "I don't know." No one explained anything further to me. I did not think of it much. I thought the soldier must have lost his way; it's easy to mix up those houses, as they all looked more or less the same.

Later, I understood. It is possible that just the sight of me—a skinny young girl, lying beside her mother—was enough to make him change his intentions. Or perhaps Aunt Anna's words were persuasive. It has been said that Russians take a kind view toward children, so this is the interpretation I would prefer.

But it is also possible my aunt sacrificed herself. She was a very goodhearted person. I will never know. It never seems the right time to ask those things, and then suddenly it is too late and, sadly, people you loved are gone.

• • • • •

Whatever the terror of that night, it did not deter Mama, Maxi, and I from pursuing our mission the next morning. We rose early, determined to walk the entire sixty kilometers back to Vienna in a single day. For conveyance we loaded all the parcels and packages that we had traded for onto a little open wagon (a *Leiterwagen*) that had upright, thin wooden bars on each side to hold things in place. With twine lashed between the bars to prevent parcels of potatoes, beets, and other vegetables from falling onto the road, we set off before sunrise, tugging the top-heavy cart past fields and farmhouses on the road to Vienna.

The overburdened cart was not up to the challenge. Before morning was out, one wheel fell off. We struggled along on three wheels for a while, bracing up the corner that constantly threatened to plunge our supplies into the dust. Then a second wheel went. Clearly it was useless continuing with the wagon. It had become more of a burden than accessory.

We stuffed our rucksacks full to bursting, loaded them on our backs, and strapped other bundles to our shoulders and sides. Our crippled wagon, now empty, was abandoned on the side of the road. The load I now carried felt excruciatingly heavy. But I'm sure it was nothing compared to the weight carried by Mama and Maxi.

Along the way, we had only one reprieve from our long-distance march. We were overtaken by a Russian soldier driving a horse-drawn wagon. Mama called out to him in Croatian—would he please give us a lift? I'm sure he saw no monetary advantage in being a Good Samaritan. The three of us—dusty, red-faced, and exhausted—were obviously impoverished. But (once again) a look at the pitiable skinny girl seemed to sway him and he indicated this to my mother, saying (in Russian) words that she interpreted as, "Only because I feel sorry for this little girl am I taking you along." At the same time, he impressed on us what a risk he was taking by proffering such kindness, since Russian military were not allowed to take Austrians onto their vehicles.

It turned out to be a short ride. When the Russian turned off the main road, we wearily disembarked, loaded up, and resumed our trek. We continued on at a discouraging pace, feeling utterly exhausted, counting each village we passed as another hurdle while numbering the ones that still lay ahead. Many people on the road were in the same predicament, forced to travel by foot from town to town.

Coming into one village, we found people literally celebrating in the streets. Today, this is my only clue to the date when we made our long march from Antau to Vienna. It must have been May 8, 1945. The news had just come through on radios in towns throughout Austria. The war was over, not just for us, but for the rest of Europe as well. It had really, truly ended.

That news was like an injection, bringing new strength to our bodies—and for a while, the lifting of our spirits was renewed at every village where people had turned out in celebration. But even this was not enough to compensate for our aching muscles and wounded feet. On the outskirts of Vienna, Mama's strength finally gave out. With a few, last stumbling steps, she settled down by the side of the road, tearfully announcing she could go no further. When she took off her shoes and socks, we saw why. Her feet were covered with blisters. We had covered most of the distance; there was only a short way to go. But her final reserves of strength were gone. She had done as much as she could. The closeness of our destination meant that, somehow, we would all make it—along with the precious food we had carried so many miles. But for the moment, she could go no farther.

We considered the situation. There was no way to lighten her load. Maxi was carrying as much as he possibly could, and I, like Mama, was nearing the end of my strength. The only alternative was to leave her there with her load, along with some of mine, while Maxi and I proceeded on. Then my brother planned to return and escort Mama home with the remaining goods.

Upon reaching our apartment, we found that Lilly was famished. She had finished all the bread and was getting by merely on black coffee. Maxi turned around almost immediately while Lilly and I began sorting the relief supplies. Soon we were all together again.

The grueling journey had been worth it. We would not go hungry.

CHAPTER 23

Frau Deutsch, the Boss—a Tragedy

I REALIZE THERE ARE SO MANY STORIES OF THOSE who perished that it lies beyond all our powers to comprehend the cost of this war. It is impossible to measure the weight of one story against another. Even so, there is one story from that period that I regard as one of the saddest. It is about Max's wartime boss, Frau Deutsch.

The income from Maxi's employment in the munitions factory had been essential to our family's survival. For Max, as I have explained, it was literally what saved his life—since, without the factory job and the intervention of Frau Deutsch on his behalf, he most certainly would have been recruited for the Nazi Organisation Tod ("Organization Death"), sent to the front, and been starved to death digging ditches or executed by the SS.

While my family could never, even for a moment, doubt Frau Deutsch's high regard for Max—and we knew how she had rescued him from certain death—we always had to wonder about her Nazi Party connections, despite Max's quick pronouncement that she was opposed to the Hitler regime. It was no secret that she would put on the Party pin and salute authorities with the required "Heil Hitler" whenever necessary. And, of course, her factory was supplying munitions to the Nazi troops. We doubted that any of this was the result of willing participation; we were almost certain it was all show, but who could know for sure? There *was* the exchange of copper sulfate—used in her factory for the galvanizing of the U-boat cannons. Max obtained copper sulfate from Frau Deutsch to trade for food from the country. We secretly traded this to our relatives on the farm, who used the rare commodity to spray their vineyards.

What went unquestioned, however, was her affection for Maxi. Though he was essentially a forced-labor employee with a questionable status and no professional qualifications, Frau Deutsch always treated him with absolute dignity.

After the war was over, when we were once again making visits to the farm and bringing home extra food, Frau Deutsch was among the first people Max was going to visit. As he had done so often before, my brother wanted to bring her some of the food we brought back from the country. He rode by Stadtbahn—this time, not to the factory, which was closed since the war's end, but directly to Frau Deutsch's apartment.

Max described what followed. He first rang the doorbell. When there was no response, he knocked loudly. Still, no reply. *Well,* he first thought, *Frau Deutsch is not home.*

As Max was about to leave, a neighbor, probably hearing the knocking, appeared at the door and asked who it was he was looking for. Max explained to the neighbor that he had worked for Frau Deutsch, that they were friends, and he had something to deliver to her.

"This is the apartment of Frau Deutsch, am I right?" Max asked.

"Yes," the neighbor confirmed, "this was her apartment."

"What do you mean? Where is she?" After Maxi had convinced her that he was Frau Deutsch's former employee and now her friend, the woman started to tell him what happened. Frau Deutsch had committed suicide, the neighbor told him. She had "turned on the gas stove and died."

The neighbor explained: Throughout the war Frau Deutsch had kept a secret from everyone. She had been married to a Jewish man. She had been successful in hiding him all those years in the apartment. The Gestapo never suspected. When the war ended, Herr Deutsch decided to leave her. That was when she took her own life.

I will never forget the expression on Max's face when he returned that day. His face was white and his eyes filled with tears as he began to tell us the sad news he had heard from Frau Deutsch's neighbor. What was originally planned as a jubilant visit to the woman who saved his life, someone he had expected to be a lifelong friend, became a tale of tragedy. I know how deeply I felt the loss myself. I could not forget all the times I had brought lunch to Max at work and seen this beautiful woman, always wearing lipstick, who would call out to him, "Maxiiiii! Your sister is here with lunch!"

Now we started to understand all. Her membership in the Nazi party, the wearing of the Party pin, and the greeting of "Heil Hitler!" had all been a necessary charade. In the end, she had lost what she most wanted and protected for so long, risking her life every day.

My eyes still fill with tears whenever I think of this elegant lady.

CHAPTER 24

New Beginnings

TODAY, IT IS HARD FOR ME TO WRITE ABOUT MAXI without having tears in my eyes, because he too is no longer with us. Throughout the war years, I had come to have simple trust that Maxi would always find a way to provide for us, protect us, rescue us from our troubles, keep the family together, and guide us forward. It was a trust that he earned many times over. I can never forget how much we depended on him and what he did for us and the heavy load we put on this man who then really was only a boy.

In 1945 the war was over, but for Max there was no chance to reclaim a lost boyhood. He simply continued, as he always had, to assume responsibility for our family's survival and welfare.

As a child, I was too young to appreciate the full measure of the responsibilities that he had borne during the war. Maxi was only a boy when he took over the heavy load of trying to replace our father. At the end of the war, he was scarcely twenty-one years old. But his youth did not seem to matter. He was purposeful and determined in everything he undertook on our behalf while, through all those war years, his own survival was hanging constantly by a string that could snap at any moment, sending him to his death.

Max, ca. 1941.

Our Maxi had the kind of self-assurance that seemed to allow him to bear responsibility without complaint. It is typical of him, and emblematic of his character, that opera, chess-playing, and reading remained a staple of his diet throughout those years, a diet as essential to him as physical nourishment. Some of those who met him in later years were brought up short by his brusque self-assurance. But it was not arrogance or snobbery that made him the way he was. (Indeed, those would have been signs of insecurity, and Maxi was as far from being insecure as any person I have ever known.) He was just a straightforward person. What seemed to inspire him most, and give him a sense of purpose, was a very elemental desire to feed his intellectual tastes while he moved steadily, unhesitatingly forward in deciding what was most important and what needed to be done next. Maxi always seemed to have a new goal in range before the rest of the family quite awoke to the fact that he was making plans. He would have done anything for his mother and two sisters. And he remained the same until the end of his life.

Of course, natural charm didn't hurt—and Maxi had that to spare. Nor did it hurt that he was good looking, well spoken, and quite attractive to women. I am sure, for instance, that Frau Deutsch's altruistic feelings played a part in rescuing Maxi from the OT, but I also think the plain fact is that she simply adored Maxi. She had no children of her own. (And how much did the circumstances of her own personal life, which she kept so highly secret until after the war, play a part in the friendship and protectiveness she showed him? Perhaps she was thinking that she could have had a son like our Max.)

Similarly, I know how, and why, the family of Robert Segen held Max in high esteem. My brother would remain close friends with Robert both during and after the war, and I came to understand that the Segens practically regarded him almost as one of their own family.

Though Lilly and I were too young to admire Max in the way so many adults seemed to, it was natural we would look upon him as a father figure throughout the war and afterwards. We listened to him and responded the way we would have listened to our own father—though I must admit we could sometimes be willful rather than fully compliant. Our mother's admiration for Max was simply boundless. Whenever she could, she bragged about him—a habit that continued throughout her lifetime.

I have already mentioned the power that Maxi had to lift our spirits during those long nights in our cold, ill-lit apartment, but I must return to it again, as this is a memory that will never leave me.

· · · · ·

I loved my mother dearly, but looking back, I realize how anxious it had made us all, during those war years, whenever she began to get "into a certain state." Often she would begin to talk about some topic that had her filled with despair. Dwelling on some neighbor's comment, she would begin to wonder whether we would be arrested and deported tomorrow. She worried constantly about our scant supply of food and money. Any knock on the door would put her into a state of frenzy. She could begin dwelling on news of the war, or the prospect that we might go on living like this for years and years. When it came to fretting about the documents needed for our protection, she would become almost overwrought, moving them from one place to another, always wanting to make sure we would have them ready in case an inspection came. This, in turn, led to moments of even greater distress: more than once, she could not remember where she had put the documents because she hid them away so often in so many different locations. We would all have sleepless nights until at last we found them again.

Another source of worry for her was the inventory of clothes with the sewn-on yellow stars. She constantly checked to make sure our yellow stars were in place on the clothes that hung in our closet—just as our protector had advised. Every moment, she was prepared for the inspection that never came.

I know how distressing it was to me, seeing Mama get worked up this way, and though I wanted to reassure and calm her, I felt helpless. Not so, Maxi. These were the times I have described—and remember so well—as Mama paced about, getting steadily more agitated, when Maxi would spring from his seat, pick her high up into the air, and begin spinning her around shouting and laughing. "Gold! Gold! Gold! You are Gold!"

Calling our mother "Gold"? Where did this come from? What possessed him? I have no idea. All I know is, it worked like magic. All the anxiety seemed to fly out of her as he spun her around. And of course the sight of my brother spinning Mama in the air so absurdly sent Lilly and I into gales of laughter. Then Mama was laughing, too, and shouting, "Put me down, Maxi! Put me down!" He did, but not until the demons of her distress had been thoroughly dispelled.

This is the brother I idolized—the Maxi who saw us safely through the war. And when the war had ended, when the city was in ruins, when we were living off bread and coffee and horse meat, is it any wonder that we all relied on Maxi to help make things right again?

$$\bullet \bullet \bullet \bullet \bullet$$

In 1945 Vienna was artfully divided by the Allies into five quadrants—Russian, British, French, American, and International. I say "artfully" because it was clear to native Viennese that the Americans and the British got the best part of the pie. Our Second District was assigned to the Russians along with the fourth, tenth, twentieth, twenty-first, and twenty-second. It was the international equivalent of gerrymandering. These were the least desirable areas of Vienna. The statesmen involved in the decision making clearly handed over to the Russians the areas of the city with the most tenements, the greatest war damage, and populated with working-class residents and immigrants of mixed nationalities who were easily intimidated by their occupiers.

As it became increasingly clear that we would not be getting on the quota for the United States any time soon, Mama and Maxi focused their efforts on finding a place for us to live in one of the more desirable areas of the city. The Third District, called Landstrasse/Hauptstrasse, was assigned to the British. But waiting lists for apartments seemed interminably long, even for the Jewish survivors, who were given preference.

It was not in Maxi's nature to put our name on a list and wait for the bureaucracy. He had met a woman from Trieste (a former possession of Austria) who was intent on returning to her home country. She owned a nice apartment in the Third District, the British zone. If she had listed it with the authorities, I am sure someone ahead of us in the queue of applicants would have gotten the apartment before us. But, again, here was someone who liked my brother's way. With little apparent effort he persuaded her to accept some "relief money" for letting us have the apartment. It was often customary after the war to pay some "relief money" in order to obtain an available apartment more quickly.

It was an arrangement that required a great deal of trust on both sides, but this was precisely the kind of situation in which my brother excelled. Within months we had moved into our beautiful new home in the Third District, Bechardgasse 5, leaving behind forever the storefront apartment at Herminengasse 15/1 that had been our war shelter.

• • • • •

Maxi's other great endeavor was to arrange for the resumption of education for his sisters and himself. During the war years, he had continued to teach me some reading and math, and I had also received lessons from Herr Schloegl. For a time I attended—briefly and secretly—some classes at a temporary place in what we called the "Temple School" (previously a Jewish center). But apart from these attempts to continue my education, I had missed out on formal schooling in the years from 1939 to 1945.

Maxi determined that I most likely belonged in the second grade of the *Gymnasium*, the advanced high school for students who would likely go on to university. Because I lacked the number of years of formal education, I was two years older than the other students in my class.

Lilly, though older than I, had fallen farther behind in her studies, and Max arranged for her to attend a high school where she would have the option of learning a trade or (if she passed certain exams) going on to the *Gymnasium*. She took the choice of a trade and became an excellent seamstress. It perfectly fit with the talent she had already shown, and by the time she finished at the high school, she could design and sew almost any clothing.

As for Max, his self-education had prepared him thoroughly to enter the *Handelsschule*—an undergraduate school for economics. After graduating, he went on to the University of Economics (*Hochschule fuer Welthandel*) and earned the title

Diplom-Kaufmann—the equivalent of a masters degree in economics. (In Austria it is not unusual to use your earned title before your name. His title was "Dkfm. Maximilian Bauer," and he could be addressed as "Herr Diplomkaufmann Bauer," which sounded quite normal for Austria, where titles are still being used since the emperor's time.)

The only delay in Max's rapid education resulted from his popularity among the new young Jewish students at the university. He was elected to become the first president after the war of the *Juedischen Hochschuelerschaft,* the Jewish University Student Council. This was a great honor.

As proud as we were of Max, at the time we were less than thrilled by his elevated rank. It meant he would remain a student just that much longer, and meanwhile we were scraping to get by in spite of our meager Holocaust survivor pensions.

CHAPTER 25

My New Life

ATTENDING SCHOOL, EATING WELL, IMPROVING my wardrobe, and, last but not least, my parents' genes of good looks all eventually had a beneficial effect on my appearance. I was still slim and (compared to Lilly) certainly not curvaceous, but by age sixteen or seventeen I could begin to see in the mirror what Frau Churan had assured me would happen—that I might have some real potential for good looks.

Of course, Lilly was still "the beauty" in the family, and many eyes were upon her as she approached marriageable age. By the end of the war, the romance between "Willie and Lilly" (much talked about in Herminengasse 15) was long over. I am quite certain she saw no more of Willie after we and most other Jewish families moved out. (In fact, I was the one who remained in contact with Willie after the war: to this day I regularly stay in touch with him and his family.) I don't know exactly how Willie measured up in my mother's eyes, but I do know Mama was quite happy when, later on, Lilly became enamored with Leo, the son of one of Vienna's premier bakers (exactly the one from which Maxi removed the sack of flour).

Mama had dreamed of—and said, many times—that she wished her daughters would marry the sons of factory owners. (And the very *best* match, in her view, would be the *Jewish* son of a factory owner!) In Austria factory owners were as highly regarded as lawyers or doctors for "marriage material." A factory owner's son was sure to be well educated and well travelled. With a family business to inherit, his prosperous future was assured. In my mother's eyes a bakery was as good as a factory. When Lilly caught the eye of Leo, whose father eventually owned more than thirty patisseries *(Konditorei)* around Vienna, Mama felt as if her dream was close to being realized. (Only "close," because Leo was not Jewish.)

But the relationship did not last. By some accounts Lilly dropped Leo—though perhaps it was the other way around. In any case, when they parted, my mother's hopes were dashed. (As it turned out, that may have been just as well. The girl who became Leo's first wife was a schoolmate of mine; they divorced, and many years after the war, I learned that Leo's fortunes suffered a serious decline—and the large family business came upon hard times and eventually went out of business.)

I lagged far behind Lilly in experiencing, or knowing how to handle, the attentions of young men. The school I attended after the war was an all-girls' *Gymnasium* offering me no opportunities to meet boys. The venue where I would finally gain confidence was the *Hakoah*. This was a Jewish sports club that had flourished before the war, home to a championship football club and to accomplished women swimmers like Judith Deutsch, Ruth Langer, and Lucie Goldner. As Vienna came to life and Jews from other parts of the world began to arrive, the Sport Club Hakoah Wien was revived and again became a gathering place for Jewish youth. (I myself was quite athletic and became one of their best women hurdlers. I was chosen to participate in the first Macabiad in Israel after the war. But my first real romance, George, took precedence and I declined participation.)

Especially popular were Saturday night dances. With all the impromptu training my mother had given me, I had become a proficient dancer, especially when it came to waltzing. Partners appeared almost instantly whenever a waltz number was struck up by the student orchestra. I had complete confidence in my ability to follow the steps of a waltz with its right and left turns. Self-consciousness vanished as soon as the music began.

Before long, I won attention from a student saxophone player who used to come over and talk to me during his breaks. It never went beyond that. Like so many other Jewish youth of the time, he had no real intention of staying in Vienna. There were still too many memories of all the people who had perished in the war, and a lack of confidence and skepticism of present-day Austrians. As soon as my saxophone player's Australian visa came through, he left for that country, and hopefully still lives there, still dancing the waltz.)

It may seem like it took some convincing, but before long I began to accept that young men were attracted to me. And, apparently, not all guys required the full-figured look that was considered ideal at that time.

It was not until the age of seventeen that I had my first romance. After the war, Vienna became a stopover for Jewish survivors to start a new life elsewhere. George was a young man who had joined a movement led by young Jews trying to convince others to immigrate to Israel. I would eventually marry this young man. In my mother's view, moving to Israel was not "her cup of tea," and she conveyed this to us often: "All you will do there is flatten stones!" she warned, envisioning that the first arrivals would be sentenced to the equivalent of hard labor as the first step toward nation building. But I did have a wonderful time dancing and socializing at the weekly get-together with all the kids who would eventually be going to Israel or to some other country that accepted immigrants.

George had a riveting story to tell—part of the reason that I began to fall in love with him. During the war, his father had been taken away by the Nazis and had never returned. His mother remarried, and the family tried to escape from Budapest by crossing the Austrian border. They were caught by Hungarian gendarmes (police) and questioned. "Where are you going?" They delivered the prepared reply, "We are hiking." That story fell apart immediately when they were asked to open their rucksacks and display the contents. "You are going *hiking*—with your best Sunday suit and best Sunday shoes?" Sure enough, they were arrested and incarcerated for a time. Upon their release, they made a second attempt with the assistance of a professional guide, and succeeded in crossing the border into Austria.

CHAPTER 26

America

THE STORY OF MY LIFE IN AMERICA IS A SEPARATE one, but it is a good one—though I only give a glimpse of that here.

I was nineteen years old when I left Vienna for Bremerhafen, Germany, to board the military ship USNS *General M. L. Hersey,* which transported European refugees to America.

MS. „GENERAL M. L. HERSEY"

The military ship USNS General M. L. Hersey. *This is a picture postcard I sent to my mother on December 12, 1951, as I was about to board the ship that would take me to the United States.*

The ship arrived in New York on Christmas Day 1951. Since it was the Christmas holiday, nobody worked, so we could not disembark until the next day. I had a whole day to stare at the Statue of Liberty and magnificent downtown New York from our boat.

Max's best friend, Fred, who had immigrated to the United States a couple of years earlier, picked me up at the dock. I was soon in touch with Cousin Else and Martin, and they took me under their wing. They arranged for me to live with an Austrian family in Washington Heights in Manhattan, and they got me my first job, working in a plastics factory. Soon the manager felt sympathy for me, as I kept burning my hands on the heat-sealing machine. He arranged for me to work in the office in a clerical position. I was surrounded by the factory owners, the management, and the office girls. My new girlfriends from Brooklyn explained the concept of the "lunch hour," with which I was unfamiliar. They also taught me that I should dress differently every day. In Vienna, I would wear the same dress to school all week. I tried to improve upon the English I had learned in *Gymnasium* in Vienna. Although I soon discovered that, since the office girls were all locals, I was learning the language with a Brooklyn accent! I came to thoroughly enjoy my surroundings and my new job, and to love American culture and food, especially hamburgers and Coca-Cola. Wanting to become more American, I even changed the spelling of my first name from Katharina to Catherine for a time.

Me in New York in the 1950s, when I was in my early twenties.

I continued to work in the plastics factory until I was ready to join George in Brazil, where he had immigrated. But I knew I would eventually return to this country, which I had quickly grown to love. I married George in São Paulo; at the time, my mother was dying of breast cancer back in Vienna with only Maxi by her side, and to this day, the thought is very painful that I left Vienna at age nineteen and never saw her again. I think of her almost every day.

I had obtained a U.S. green card, and this enabled me to bring my new husband back to the United States. In 1954 we both relocated to New York, where we found jobs. While living in Brazil, George had worked importing goods for his clients from the United States; living in New York, he now exported goods from the States to Brazil to those same clients. I worked as a German/English–speaking secretary; this ultimately turned out to be a temporary job as George's business took off quickly. But with the advent of the Korean War, he was suddenly called into the American army. Now I had to take over his business and try to run it for the next two years until his discharge. So I found myself, at age twenty-three, dealing with businessmen three times my age while George was giving me almost daily instructions from a public telephone booth on the army base. The calls became fewer as I gained experience and confidence. The business survived and became a successful, well-known entity after George's return from the army—but our marriage did not. Perhaps we were just too young and married too soon. In any event, though the marriage ended, we have two wonderful daughters and four incredible grandchildren. George remarried quickly but, unfortunately, his second wife passed away recently. He does, however, have lovely stepchildren and step-grand-children. They surround him frequently, and together with our children we often celebrate holidays together in one of our family homes.

• • • • •

For many years I was a single woman raising two daughters. During this time I went back to school at Hunter College and studied art history. I also dabbled at painting a bit as a hobby. I held an administrative position at Polyclinic Hospital, but that ended when the hospital was forced to close. I started to look for a job connected to art, and in 1977, I became the director of an art gallery in SoHo. At the time, that part of New York City was just beginning to garner attention as the new art district. Right from the start, I loved what I was doing and it was to be the beginning of a lifelong career. However, I often worked six days a week, and my sister warned me that I was spending too many hours and too many days at work, and I would never find a man again who would put up with my busy schedule.

Yet one day a couple came into the gallery to view our exhibition of a Mexican artist. I was admiring this particularly handsome couple, and the thought went through my mind that I had been single for quite a few years, and I was thinking how nice it would be to once again be part of a couple. We engaged in conversation about art, especially the present exhibition. The gentleman, who was a physician, and his lady friend spent a good deal of time with me. Apparently, the doctor had fallen in love with a painting hanging on the wall named *Prelude* and decided to buy it. It was a large oil-on-canvas with a beautiful dark-haired woman, breasts exposed, lounging in front of a bowl of fruit—reminiscent of Matisse's *Olympia*.

The next morning it was a Saturday, and much to my surprise, the handsome guy from the day before had reappeared back in the gallery, without his companion but with a tray of cakes and coffee—"because you are from Vienna," he said. Briefly disillusioned remembering the "couple" revelry of the prior day, it was hard to resist this man who paid so much attention to me. We soon found out that we had much in common. He liked art, music (especially opera), and skiing. We fell in love, and four years later, on a snowy winter day in January 1983, we married. At the writing of this memoir, we recently celebrated our thirtieth wedding anniversary at the same country inn where we got married. And the painting *Prelude* still hangs prominently on our bedroom wall.

Bill and I celebrating our thirtieth anniversary.

• • • • •

With the encouragement of my "collector" husband, I opened my own fine arts gallery, the Katharina Rich Perlow Gallery, in 1984. After thirty-three years in the art business, I decided to officially close the gallery's doors in 2011 so that Bill and I could spend more time together, especially on weekends, as I worked most Saturdays for so many years.

CHAPTER 27

The People in My Memoir

OVER THE YEARS I HAVE TRIED TO KEEP TRACK OF many of the friends and relatives who played a part in this memoir.

• • • • •

On my father's side there was my intrepid Aunt Rosa, who returned from Portugal after the war to reclaim her house and country store. She was already seventy years old when she reopened the store and continued to manage it until the age of eighty-two. She died at the age of eighty-six.

• • • • •

Of our early friends from Wiener Neustadt, the Buchsbaum family, none of them survived. Frau Buchsbaum (our seamstress), Herr Buchsbaum, Max, Julie (Lilly's childhood friend), and Fritzi (my early admirer) all died in the gas chambers.

• • • • •

Long after the war, during Max's seasonal visits to Vienna, he often visited with our protector, Herr Segen, and his son. Herr Segen was imprisoned for some time after the war on charges relating to his association with the German authorities. After his release, he resumed his career and became one of the most celebrated attorneys in Europe. His son, also an attorney, joined his father in the law practice. Despite Max's close friendship with the family, I believe they never discussed the wartime activities of the father. Herr Segen lived to be ninety years old.

•••••

Our neighbors and friends who were deported from Herminengasse 15 never returned to Vienna. I never learned what became of them. One assumes they died in the gas chambers or from starvation or illnesses.

•••••

I maintained a close relationship with Frau Sidie and her family. Visiting Vienna, I invariably went to see her. My husband, Bill, was taken, as I was, with the warmth of this lady. During one of our last visits, she whispered to Bill to "take good care of Ketl" (as she called me). She died in her nineties, living out her last few years with her son and his family. I continue to visit Willie and his family during every one of my Vienna visits.

From right: Me, Willie, and his wife, Karin.

Willie, who is now eighty-six, is still very handsome and in good health. He has been married more than fifty years to the same lady, and they have one son. He knows the love and admiration I always felt for his mother. I look at her as a hero and I am grateful for having known her.

• • • • •

After Herr Klein—the man found hiding in Frau Sidie's apartment at the time of the building's raid—fled to the home of the gentile woman of Frau Sidie's suggestion, an informer discovered his hideout and reported it to the Gestapo. Herr Klein was promptly seized and deported, never to return. It can only be assumed that he did not survive his ordeal. The woman who took him in was also arrested, and sent to the Bergen-Belsen concentration camp for harboring a Jew. Though she survived and returned to Vienna, neither Frau Sidie nor Willie would hear from her again. As far as they could tell, she wanted no further contact with them.

· · · · ·

About twenty-five years ago, my husband and I visited Frau Kopica in Vienna. (It was Frau Kopica's husband who had been so courageous in saving the lives of all of us who were hidden in the cellar in the last days before liberation.) Frau Kopica and her family were living in the same apartment at Herminengasse 15. She was suffering from what seemed to be liver cancer. (My husband, Bill, is a doctor who specializes in gastroenterology and was able to advise her about some treatment.) Frau Kopica told us that her daughter, Ditta, whom Lilly and I loved as a child, had no contact with the family. I wanted to know more, but hesitated to ask after these remarks.

I wish I could also have seen Herr Kopica on that visit—we had so much to thank him for!—but he was not at home at the time. We have never managed to contact them since that trip.

• • • • •

Aunt Sarah, Uncle Bernhard, and cousins Martin and Else all lived into old age in New York. Throughout my time in the United States, I saw them frequently, and Else was like a mother to me, giving me much good advice during her lifetime.

Cousin Eric, who lost his father to the Nazis at age three, became a social worker for the City of New York. He married a woman who is a violinist; she and Eric have three grown children, and I love to visit them.

• • • • •

Lilly got married in Vienna at age twenty-one. She married Al, a young man also from a mixed marriage (father Jewish, mother gentile), who survived the war with his parents. She and her husband left for the United States in 1952. Married for more than sixty years, they have two daughters and five grandchildren. Al is an engineer and Lilly is a homemaker, and for more than thirty years she has done volunteer work at their local hospital in New Jersey, where they have settled.

*Max and Lilly console Mama as Lilly departs for the
United States. The caption on the back of this photo,
written in 1952, translates as "Mommy-love, you make the
'sweetest' face. Well, it is a Farewell, isn't it, Lilly."*

• • • • •

Maxi remained with Mama in the apartment he had found for us
in the third district of Landstrasse/Hauptstrasse. After the war,
during the occupation of the Allies, jobs were extremely limited,
especially for a young economist. But as long as Mama was alive,
Maxi would not leave the country without her. They were both
waiting for the Austrian quota to come through so they could join
us. Both Lilly and I wrote home frequently, and the responses
from Mama, usually transcribed by Max, always expressed

happiness in hearing from her daughters. As time slipped away, we all looked forward to the day when Mama and Max would be able to make the long-awaited trip to America to settle here with us. But if there was one thing that never changed in my mother's character, it was her desire to protect her children. As she grew older, this would mean protecting them from the truth about her own declining health. Maxi knew long before we did that Mama had metastatic cancer. But he was unfailingly loyal, and if Mama wanted it kept from us, he would carry out her wish. From the letters that reached us, neither her children nor any of her other relatives on the other side of the ocean suspected how serious her condition was. (Only much later did I know that Maxi had learned how to administer morphine injections to make her final days easier.) Mama, the woman Maxi always called "Gold," who had fulfilled her wish to bring us through the war alive, died of cancer in Vienna in 1953 at the age of sixty-one, without ever seeing her daughters again.

With my own grief and sorrow came a myriad of other feelings—anger (even at Maxi!), regret, and remorse. But as time passed, what I longed for was for her to somehow know what happened afterward. And what I regret most in my life—and this pain, sadly, never leaves me—is that I was not able to say goodbye to my mother. I saw her last when I was only nineteen years old. I still think of the scent from the Wiener Neustadt's Apotheke crème, and it reminds me of what she went through to bring us through the war alive.

• • • • •

After Mama died, George and I made an extended business trip to São Paulo, Brazil, and we invited Max to come visit us as he was now living alone in Vienna without family. Austria was still occupied by the Russians, and life improved very slowly. Max wasn't in Brazil long before he decided to stay and find work. He found a position as an economist with an international firm, and remained with the same employer for the next forty years. He never married.

After retirement, during the last ten years of his life, Maxi divided his time between Vienna and São Paulo, enjoying the "reversed" cultural seasons in each country. Winters in Vienna, he became a fixture at the Hotel Post, where everybody knew and loved him. During the Brazilian winters, he lived in São Paulo. In both countries, he pursued his love for opera, concerts, and other cultural events.

Besides speaking five languages, Max was one of the most well-read persons you could hope to meet. You could talk about nearly any subject with him, and he would have some insight or reflection to offer.

Frequently, my brother visited Lilly and me and our families in the United States, always showering his sisters and our children with gifts. He adored all of us, and vice versa. He would call us every Sunday morning around breakfast time from Brazil or Vienna, depending on where he was. His penchant for frugality never changed! How typical of Max that he would calculate what he could save by using phone cards rather than a home line.

Despite his great care with expenses, Max's one great passion would make him break all rules of frugality. He would spend anything for an air ticket transporting him to a city where the opera singer Maria Callas or another of his favorite divas was performing. And when it happened that Maria Callas "lost her voice" and missed a performance, Max took it personally and would phone us from whatever country he had flown to. The first words over the phone would be "the bitch cancelled on me again."

Maxi died on May 6, 2011, in Vienna, at age eighty-six, of vascular disease. His vibrant intellect, even at the end, enabled him to continue to have intelligent and timely conversations with those who visited him. Reading the daily newspaper, he even kept up with the latest cultural reviews, advising us which plays we should see. During this period, most of our family flew to Vienna to visit him. After all, he was not only special as a brother, he was also a special uncle to our children. Max's vast knowledge and warmth attracted the children, and they loved being around him. His absence leaves an emptiness in my husband's heart as well. Bill misses the long, wonderful conversations he used to have with Max. There was just something about him—his direct nature, his kindness, and even the way he dressed—these all made him the unique, humorous, and generous individual he was.

During his three-month hospitalization in Vienna, we visited twice. I last saw Maxi just a few days before he died. I did not want to miss out again as with Mama. I have learned how fast people can be pulled from you without warning.

Maxi is buried in Vienna's Jewish Cemetery, where we spent so many days during the war; his grave is very close to my parents' graves. His death leaves me and my sister inconsolable. And on Sunday mornings, there's a vacuum as we wait for his calls that no longer come.

Max in 2010.
Photograph taken by
Monica Rich Kosann.

CHAPTER 28

Returning to Vienna

I HAVE MADE MANY RETURN VISITS TO AUSTRIA, AND each time I go, my first stop is the Jewish cemetery where my father, mother, and Max are buried.

Schanko, my cousin on my mother's side, is still living in Zagersorf in the same house where my mother was born. His "little" sister, Maritza—who was so dear to me—died suddenly of pancreatic cancer in 2008. Whenever I visit Vienna, I never fail to make the trip to the country where we spent so many hours during the war, and which saved us from starvation.

• • • • •

The famous Vienna Prater, with its pony carousel where I once tended the horses and collected fares, looks today almost exactly the way it did in the war years. It is still owned by the same family, the Reinprechts, who operated it when I was a young girl.

When Bill and I paid a visit a number of years ago, it was all very familiar. I am sure the pipe organ in the center and the elaborate carriages have been through many phases of restoration, and the well-groomed, dappled ponies are many generations removed from the ones I led around, but every detail is just as splendid as it looked in my days there.

And there was a familiar face, as well. Maria, the daughter who is my age, still runs the business. She is living in the same house where the Reinprecht family has always lived, located right behind the carousel. It was obvious from our conversation that she took immense pride in maintaining the family business. She showed us the immaculate stables and horses—it seems to be her life. Her parents and one sister had died.

I asked Maria if she remembered me.

"Of course!" she exclaimed. "You were very good with the children. My parents often mentioned it."

I then had the opportunity to ask her the question that had haunted me for decades. During the time I was at the carousel—when I had to keep pretending that, like her, I was a regular school attendee—did she ever know I was Jewish?

"No," Maria, replied. "I had no idea. It is possible my parents knew, but if so, they never told us children."

· · · · ·

In years past, during repeated visits to Vienna, Bill and I would occasionally walk in the neighborhood where I lived during the war. The Second District was an area that had not kept pace with the growth of the rest of the city. It remained a district given over to newly arrived immigrants from other countries. During our walks, we occasionally stopped at Herminengasse 15, but the entrance door was always kept locked, and I was hesitant about ringing the bell.

Recently, however, that area of Vienna has undergone a kind of renaissance. The Second District, where rents have been cheap, has become a student area, and young people have breathed new life into the neighborhood. The city has conferred the honor of opening a new subway stop with a station called "Herminengasse." Cafes and wine bars line the street near the station and throughout the Second District.

In June 2011, I decided to knock on the door of my old apartment, number 1, at Herminengasse 15, where I had spent such a big part of my childhood. I wanted to see what it felt like to revisit the place of our survival.

The sign on the door read "Soma Architects." Right away I felt better about ringing the bell as, apparently, the place was now a business rather than a private residence. A young man opened the door. I told him that I had spent the war years there, and would he mind if I took a look at the apartment for the sake of my memories? He immediately invited us in.

I was in for a real surprise.

The place was completely unrecognizable. It had been transformed into a high-tech architect's office, with white walls and track lighting. The storefront doors as well as the door to the little courtyard had been changed by the installation of large, modern windows. What had once been our kitchen was now a fancy foyer leading to the main office (our formerly unlivable storeroom). The area that had served as our bedroom/living room was filled with modern office furniture and looked like a conference room. The young architects stopped working at their computers when I began to tell some of my story.

These young people had no idea what had happened in this building before they were born. Two of them were particularly interested. They were quite surprised when I described the events that occurred in this building. They had moved into the building as students because it was cheap living in the Second District. By the time they graduated, the district had changed dramatically and they were able to rent "our" apartment, transforming it into the high-tech office and showroom it is now. During all the time they had been there, they had no idea of its prior history.

Since this meeting, we have continued to exchange some emails. They recently sent me their book, entitled *Soma: One Ocean*, featuring the incredible architectural work they have done in places around the globe—all created in our old apartment at Herminengasse 15.

EPILOGUE

As I finish this memoir, I have in my hand a postcard from a young woman living in America written to her mother in Vienna. I cannot look at it now without my eyes blurring with tears. On the front of the postcard is a photograph of the ship that brought me to New York. On the reverse are the words in German I wrote to my mother, sister, and brother when I was on my way to the United States at age nineteen. The card begins "My dearest Mamalein."

I know that when I wrote those words I was young and filled with excited expectations about my future. In front of me was a life that was still unknown. But whatever lay ahead, I was certain it would be better than my childhood. I was already seeing parts of the world I had never imagined. And looking back, I can say that most, if not all, of my expectations have been fulfilled. I was soon to be wonderfully reunited with family members I thought I might never see again. I would meet people who were as filled with energy and curiosity as I was. I also hoped Mama, Max, and Lilly would soon be able to join me.

I now wonder how many postcards, letters, and telegrams— much like mine—must have been flooding the world at that time. Many came from children like me, older or younger, saying fare-well to parents they had left behind. In those postwar years, in the turmoil that followed, there were mothers and fathers reaching out to their children; friends seeking friends, hoping to be reunited; siblings, separated by war, making discoveries about who had survived, learning the tragedies of those who had not; and millions more, searching for those who were separated or lost.

•••••

There comes a time, I know, when survivors are asked by others—or ask themselves—whether their experiences and losses have left lasting scars.

For me, those terrifying moments in the catacombs during air raids and, in the final seven days of the war, in the cellar of our building, are never to leave me. To this day I am very claustrophobic. I feel faint if I am in a small room with no window or if I am riding in an elevator and the doors do not open quickly. Airplanes are not easy for me, and whenever I fly I have to psychologically prepare myself for the feelings I will experience when the door closes, the plane lifts off, and I am virtually trapped among other passengers in a closed compartment. At all times I try to avoid large crowds in closed or even open spaces.

Another consequence of my war experience is that I feel immediate empathy if I see a child crying, even if it is for a minor reason (which is usually the case).

A while ago, when I was visiting a museum, I noticed a boy about six or seven years of age lagging behind his parents, who were engaged in conversation. In a moment when the parents were not paying much attention, a glass door automatically closed behind them, blocking the boy's way. The parents continued walking, certain the boy was following them, not noticing his absence. The child trapped behind the door became upset and began pounding on the locked glass door, screaming, and crying out for his father and mother.

What happened next occurred in a flash. I too was outside the door. At the sounds of screams, I turned to look, and something inside me seemed to collapse. His pounding on the door instantly reminded me of Lilly—when we were in prison and she clung to the prison window bars screaming for Mama. I rushed to the door and tried to yank it open. It would not budge either way. The boy's pounding continued, and I broke down and started to cry. I felt embarrassed in the company of friends.

As it turned out, someone on the other side was quickly able to lead the boy away from this automatically shut door, and it took only a small effort to reunite him with his parents.

It is no secret why I responded that way. I know what it means to be locked in a place where you cannot get out. The screams and cries of that helpless boy evoked emotions in me that were so powerful, and so deeply embedded in my soul, that for a moment I was as helplessly in their grip as a six-year-old child.

My other "war inheritance" is the way I always have to maintain order with documents that are in my possession. I am obsessed with having documents in total order, and I become frantic when I can't find papers, especially the more important ones like a birth certificate, license, or passport. Just like my mother before me, I sometimes put a document in one place where I think it's safer than in another place. Then, later on, I forget where I put it because I have moved it around so much.

•••••

My mother always said, "I only want to survive the war to save my children's lives." And so she did.

In all the postcards and letters that Lilly and I sent to her from America, our words and accounts of our life really embedded a single message. Over and over again, we wanted her to know: *Mama, you succeeded, you saved our lives.*

Now, I wonder whether this memoir is perhaps the continuation—though not the end—of that message to her.

If so, I do not feel it is quite finished. There is still this to say:

> Mama, I think you recognized I was one of those children who could always find some way to be happy, no matter what was happening. That has not changed. Since the war, I have had a full and happy life. I love this country. It has given me much more than I ever expected. I love my husband and my family.

> That's what I want you to know. You wanted to save your children's lives. Well, you succeeded. And I could not be happier than I am with the life you gave me, the life you protected—the little girl you saved during times of inconceivable hardship and danger. All this is thanks to you and your son, Max, whom we all so dearly loved.

Katharina Rich Perlow

January 2013

ABOUT THE AUTHOR

Katharina Rich Perlow was born in Wiener Neustadt, Austria. She grew up in Vienna and immigrated to the United States in 1951. She attended Hunter College, studying art history, and became director of an art gallery in SoHo in 1977. In 1984 she founded her own fine arts gallery, The Katharina Rich Perlow Gallery, 1984–2011. She lives in New York City with her husband, Bill, and continues to work as a private art dealer.